D0933041

BEST OF BOOCH

SIGS Reference Library

Donald G. Firesmith
Editor-in-Chief

Additional Volumes in Preparation

BEST OF BOOCH

Designing Strategies for Object Technology

GRADY BOOCH

EDITED BY

ED EYKHOLT

SIGS
BOOKS & MULTIMEDIA

NEW YORK · LONDON · PARIS · MUNICH · COLOGNE

Library of Congress Cataloging-in-Publication Data
Booch, Grady.
    The best of Booch / Grady Booch : edited by Ed Eykholt.
        p. cm. -- (SIGS reference library series ; 8)
    Includes bibliographical references and index.
    ISBN 1-884842-71-2 (pbk.)
        1. Computer software--Development. 2. Object-oriented programming
(Computer science) 3. Booch method. I. Eykholt, Edward M., 1962– . II.
Title. III. Series.
    QA76.76.D47B65 1996
    005.1'1 -- dc20   96-45951
                                                                                                     CIP
                                                                                                      AC

PUBLISHED BY
SIGS Books & Multimedia
71 W. 23rd Street, Third Floor
New York, New York 10010
http://www.sigs.com

Copyright © 1996 by SIGS Books & Multimedia. All Rights Reserved. Neither
this book nor any part may be reproduced or transmitted in any form or by any
means, electronic or mechanical, including photocopying, microfilming, and
recording, or by any information storage and retrieval system, without permis-
sion in writing from the publisher.

Any product mentioned in this book may be a trademark of its company.

Composition by Ed Eykholt
Cover design by Brian Griesbaum
Printed on acid-free paper

SIGS Books ISBN 1-884842-71-2
Prentice Hall ISBN 0-13-739616-3

Printed in the United States of America
00 99 98 97 96   10 9 8 7 6 5 4 3 2 1
First Printing October, 1996

To Jan: My friend, my lover, my wife

— Grady

To my daughter Suzanne

— Ed

ABOUT THE AUTHORS

Grady Booch, inventor of *the Booch method* for object-oriented software engineering, is Chief Scientist at Rational Software Corporation, headquartered in Santa Clara, California. He has been with Rational since its founding in 1980. He has contributed significantly to improving the effectiveness of software development worldwide, through his seminal work in object modeling, iterative development, and software architecture.

The Booch method is being used to develop some of the most complex and demanding software systems, including air-traffic-control systems, commercial aircraft avionics, financial trading systems, telecommunication switching networks, and defense systems. Additionally, Grady developed a family of reusable components in both Ada and C++, which helped to popularize software reuse and make it economically feasible.

Grady was also involved in the development of Rational Environment, the company's original software-engineering environment and its compiler technology. Grady was also the original architect for the Rational Rose object-oriented analysis and design tool. He has worked in a variety of object-oriented and object-based languages, including Ada, C++, Smalltalk, Visual Basic, and Java.

He served as a consultant on the highly successful FS 2000 shipboard command-and-control system developed by CelsiusTech, one of Sweden's leading developers of command-and-control systems. On this project, Grady worked with the project's chief architect and trained many of the company's senior developers in applying object-oriented technology. This project became the basis of a profitable line of business for CelsiusTech and, as a result of applying Grady's methods and Rational's technology, the company has been able to reuse up to 70 percent of its code from project to project.

Grady has consulted on numerous projects worldwide, helping some organizations develop client/server systems and assisting others in customizing their own object-oriented methods. Some of his customers include the U.S. Government, Alcatel, Andersen Consulting, AT&T, MCI, Microsoft, Price Waterhouse, UBS (a large Swiss bank), the Orient Overseas Container Line (based in Hong Kong), and Xerox. Grady was also the project manager for the Range Safety Display System, a 500,000-line-of-code (LOC) application at Vandenberg Air Force Base. He was also the project engineer for a 1.5 million LOC real-time telemetry processing application there.

Grady's skill as an innovative computer scientist is matched by his skill as synthesizer, author, and popularizer on topics of object technology. Grady considers himself an architect. His books, articles, and talks have led to a great increase in the awareness and application of object technology.

This is Grady's fifth book. He has authored four books published by Benjamin/Cummings, including *Software Engineering with Ada and Software Components with Ada*. The second edition of his third book, *Object-Oriented Analysis and Design*, describes the theory, notation, process, and pragmatics of object-oriented technology. His fourth book, *Object Solutions: Managing the Object-Oriented Project*, focuses on factors affecting the effective management of OO projects.

Grady has also published more than 85 technical articles on object-oriented technology and software engineering, which appear regularly appearing in the *Report on Object Analysis and Design* (ROAD) and *Object Magazine*. Grady consults and lectures on object-oriented topics throughout the world.

Grady's experience in software engineering and OO method development paved the way to allow Jim Rumbaugh, Ivar Jacobson, and him to join forces with the express goal of unifying their respective methods (Booch, OMT, and OOSE/Objectory) into one unified definition of notation and semantics: the Unified Modeling Language (UML). The UML is expected to be embraced within the industry. Version one of the UML is anticipated to be published by early 1997.

As much as possible, Grady has remained accessible to professionals in the object-technology industry. He regularly communicates with a wide audience in the industry via e-mail, the comp.object newsgroup, and the OTUG mailing list.

Grady is a distinguished graduate of the United States Air Force Academy, where he received a B.S. in computer science in 1977. He received his M.S.

in Electrical Engineering / Computer Engineering from the University of California at Santa Barbara in 1979. He is a member of the ACM, the IEEE, Computer Professionals for Software Responsibility, and the Association for Software Design. Grady is an ACM Fellow and a Rational Fellow. He can be contacted by e-mail: *egb@rational.com*

Ed Eykholt (pronounced "eye-colt") is a sales engineer with Rational Software Corporation in McLean, Virginia, where he provides technical sales support for the Rose product line of object-oriented software engineering tools and delivers training for OO tools and methods. He was instrumental in collating feedback on the Unified Modeling Language and coordinating its standardization. With Don Firesmith he coauthored the *Dictionary of Object Technology: The Definitive Desk Reference.*

Prior to joining Rational in mid-1995, Ed was a Business Systems Consultant with NCR/AT&T in Dayton, Ohio. Ed facilitated dialog between business and information-systems professionals in order to achieve consistent understanding and expectations between them, assuring that IS supported business strategies and requirements.

He has used object-oriented analysis and design, business process reengineering, and other techniques. He has significant experience in accounting systems and product management.

Ed received his Bachelor of Science degree in Electrical Engineering in 1985 and Master of Science in Management (MBA) in 1987 from Purdue University and its Krannert School of Management, West Lafayette, Indiana. He can be contacted by e-mail: *eykholt@rational.com*

FOREWORD

I greatly admire Grady Booch's contributions to the software development community. One might look no further than what he presented in *Object Oriented Modeling and Design with Applications* and begin to appreciate his contributions. I submit, however, that the essence of the contribution is in understanding all of the complexities associated with software development, managing the risks, and delivering tangible, real-world results. My measure of real-world results is: "Did we deliver what the customer needed, on time and on budget?" Anything else is suboptimal. The Booch Method has been proven to do this, time and time again, in real projects with real deliverables in the real world.

Over the years Grady has written and spoken almost nonstop about the challenges facing those of us who call ourselves members of the software development community. Many of these talks, books, and papers have centered on the benefits of Object Technology and the Booch Method. Many others have dealt with topics less concrete and in some ways much more difficult to address or even acknowledge: risk awareness and management, balancing complexities, team dynamics, roles and responsibilities for project team members, architecture, rigor and discipline, patterns, reuse, and so on. Not only are these topics often missed by project teams, they are often ignored, leading to predictable results. I think you, the reader, will find some additional awareness from this book, or perhaps some reinforcement or embellishment for your software development practices.

At Xerox, our teams do not believe that object technology is a way to deliver systems. They believe it is the *only* way. Since establishing a competency center for OT in mid-1994, we have been evangelizing OT, the Booch method, a Methodology Framework, and a holistic, balanced set of work practices, architecture, and many of the topics listed previously. We have been working with Grady and Rational Software Corporation continuously to help us reengineer the process of delivering information systems to our customers. In fact, the "Booch book" is required reading for our software engineers. This book will join Booch's other works on our bookshelves.

Our progress is, like our software development process, iterative and incremental. For us, this work is never "done." The "surprise" of the Internet/WWW is as poignant an example as one might need to validate this approach. Our purpose is to create information systems to support the business of Xerox Corporation. We firmly believe that the technological and cultural foundations we are building in our software development community are required for a successful future. Through our work, we will partner with the business community and rapidly respond to the changing business environment. We could not even dream of this without object technology. We have committed our future to OT. This is a risk we have acknowledged and are managing. Because you are reading this book, perhaps you have come to the same conclusions, or are just frustrated with limited success with conventional approaches. In any case, read on and enjoy.

Alan F. Nugent
Vice President and CTO,
Xerox Corporation,
GP&IM Global Strategy and Advanced Technology

PREFACE

This volume contains a collection of essays on various object-oriented topics that we hope you will find interesting. These essays are based on articles published since Grady Booch's 1993 book, *Object Oriented Modeling and Design with Applications*, second edition.

Grady has written and spoken on a host of topics key to the success of the object technology industry. Obviously, Grady has written on the Booch Method, and how a complete method must address a model's notation and semantics as well as a process for creating that model. As he has observed, a method is necessary, but not sufficient, for the success of a project. The success of an object-oriented project depends on many other factors, including business, project and team dynamics, architecture, artifacts, and implementation. Over the years, Grady has addressed all of these topics and they are represented here in this collection. This book is organized according to these categories. Furthermore, the topic of managing OO projects was the focus of Grady's earlier book, *Object Solutions: Managing the Object-Oriented Project*, so we only include more recent articles on this topic here.

Because some of these articles date back as far as 1993, you may notice that some of Grady's comments about the industry, for example, may not jibe with today's landscape. We decided to leave many of these comments in as is for their historical perspective, recognizing how quickly the industry is evolving. In other areas, we felt it was especially helpful to adjust the Booch Method notation and semantics to reflect the current thinking in the Unified Modeling Language (UML). Some areas of the UML are still evolving, but most of the notation presented herein is stable, except where noted. As a editor of this book, Ed Eykholt revisited each article, adjusting it, if necessary, to assure its applicability and current thinking. Personal pronouns (I, me, my) should be interpreted as referring to Grady, with the exception of text appearing in this sans serif font, such as in the introductions for each chapter, or footnotes in brackets, [ ], which were written by Ed.

INTENDED AUDIENCE
This collection will interest software professionals who are concerned about the success of object-oriented software projects, including anyone with a

role on the project team, and students. Because the book is a collection of a broad set of topics, it need not be read in order nor in its entirety to be of value.

Many of the topics are independent of an object-oriented approach altogether, but other articles do assume a working knowledge of the OO concepts. Booch's *Object Oriented Modeling and Design with Applications* is the primary reference text for this background. Because we have updated these articles to reflect the current thinking of the Unified Modeling Language, those interested in understanding how the Booch Method has evolved into the current UML definition will find this book valuable. The latest information on the UML can be found on Rational Software's web site, *http://www.rational.com.*

We encourage you to read on about good things object oriented and the challenges facing those who search for them.

CONTENTS

CHAPTER 1

MANAGING COMPLEXITY

When Grady returned from giving the keynote address at the International Java Developers' Conference in New York City in May 1996, I remember him commenting on the euphoria surrounding Java and its promise to make distributed Internet development easy. In his keynote, he tried to temper this frenzy with the message that the development of large, distributed systems would remain a very challenging process for a long time to come. All software developers search to make software development easier, and although Java is a step in the right direction, for most systems of any size software development continues to be a fundamentally hard problem. Unfortunately, there are many developers who are in denial about this reality.

It is true that the industry is getting better at delivering large systems, but is this enough? Has this yielded an industry with predictable, mature, and stable development methods and processes? Not quite. Instead, systems have continued to grow in size and complexity, and this has clearly increased the problems of development. We include two related articles in this chapter:

- In the first article excerpt, *Coming of Age in an Object-Oriented World*,[1] Grady reflects on a moment early in his career when he realized that a trend towards software complexity would be a central challenge for a long time. This is precisely why his work has focused on ways to deal with it. In this article, he also suggests a classification of types of software and their respective roles.

- The second article, *A Question of Balance*,[2] articulates how the success of OO projects is dependent on so many factors, technical as well as nontechnical. A team's ability to strike a balance between the

---

[1] Based on Booch, G. (1994). Coming of age in an object-oriented world. *IEEE Software 11*(6).

[2] Based on Booch, G. (1995). A question of balance. *Object Magazine 5*(4).

two is an excellent predictor of likely success. This theme of balance is evident in Grady's collective works.

COMING OF AGE IN AN OBJECT-ORIENTED WORLD

One of my more vivid memories of growing up in the late 1960s—when the turn of the millennium still seemed so very far away—was sitting in a darkened theater, entranced by that classic science fiction epic, *2001: A Space Odyssey.* To a young boy's active imagination, this was truly a thing of wonder. Clarke and Kubrick wove a tale of innocent complexity that foreshadowed a number of contemporary technologies: massively parallel machines, autonomous and self-healing agents, ubiquitous networks, video conferencing, voice recognition, and data visualization. Perhaps most striking was the film's subtlety. Collectively, these complex technologies were simply a part of the movie's natural background.

The 1960s (and the '70s and much of the '80s) were a time when giants roamed the earth. *Mainframes* ruled the computing landscape, consuming vast quantities of COBOL and FORTRAN as required to fuel their comparatively small minds. Evolving underfoot and largely unnoticed were the more primitive upstart technologies of microprocessors, networks, and graphical user interfaces, whose presence would, as we realize today, forever change the rules of computing.

Although all the hardware in *2001* was delightfully exotic, I remember leaving the theater with one nagging question: *Who was going to write all that cool software?* In retrospect, I realize now that I had stumbled upon a simple but fundamental truth: *Our ability to imagine complex applications will always exceed our ability to create them.*

From the perspective of a software developer, this truth makes for very interesting times. Sophisticated software is so pervasive that it creates an insatiable demand for creative architects, abstractionists, and implementers. Consider all the software behind many of the activities that we now take for granted in an industrialized society: making a phone call, buying shares in a mutual fund, driving a car, watching a movie, having a medical examination. The underlying technology disappears, as it did in *2001* and as it does in these examples, when we have begun to master the inherent complexity.

It is not radical to predict that future software will be evolutionarily more complex. Indeed, there are two dominant forces at play that drive this trend: the *increased connectivity* of distributed computing systems and *greater user expectations* for better visualization of and access to information. The first force—increased connectivity—is made possible by the emergence of increasingly high-bandwidth conduits of information, and is made practical by economies of scale. The second force—greater user expectations—is largely a consequence of the Nintendo generation that is socially aware of the creative possibilities of automation. Under the influences of both forces, it is reasonable for a consumer to expect that a movie ordered over cable television be billed directly to his or her bank account. It is reasonable for a scientist to expect online access to information in distant laboratories. It is reasonable for an architect to expect the ability to walk through a virtual blueprint created by remote collaborators. It is reasonable for a retail business to expect there to be no seams in its mission-critical systems, connecting the event of a customer purchasing an item to the activities of the company's buyers (who react to rapidly changing consumer tastes) as well as to the activities of the company's marketing organization (who must target new offerings to increasingly specialized groups of consumers). It is those very places that we do find seams in such systems; those times when we ask "why *can't* I do *x*?" hint at the reality that we have not yet mastered the inherent complexity of a particular domain.

The world's current supply of software developers would easily be consumed just by the activities of writing software that derive from the natural consequences of these two simple forces. If we add to this equation the largely unproductive tasks of coping with the microprocessor wars, the operating system wars, the programming language wars, and even the methodology wars, we find that there are scant resources left to spend on discovering and inventing the next class of so-called killer applications. Thankfully, some of these wars are not as violent as they once were.

On the positive side, software development today is far less constrained by hardware. Compared to just a decade ago, many applications operate in a world of abundant MIPS, excess memory, and cheap connectivity. Of course, there are two sides to this blessing. On the one hand, this means that our hardware no longer must dramatically affect the shape of the software architectures that we craft. On the other hand, this embarrassment of riches tends to encourage an appetite for software that will never be satiated.

So, we are still faced with that fundamental truth of our imaginations outpacing our abilities. The consequence is that software development, as we know it today, will continue to be labor intensive. Ah, but the operative phrase in our observation is "as we know it today," and therein lies an opportunity for mitigating the stark imbalance in the supply and demand for software.

Indeed, I have seen the future, and it is object oriented.

A QUESTION OF BALANCE

A project's success is dependent on a myriad of factors. Let me begin by making two simple and related observations. First, *for an endeavor as complex as crafting a large piece of software, the failure of any one aspect of a project can cause it to blow up in your face.* In his most recent book, Capers Jones enumerates a number of such software risks, any one of which, if left untreated, can lead to disaster (Jones 1994). Second, the reverse of my first observation is not necessarily true: *No one factor of a project can ever drag it to successful closure.* Furthermore, the obsessive focus of a project on any one particular success factor is a clear sign of organizational immaturity, and as such is equally a good predictor of failure.

In my experience, there are at least four general areas of success factors that each project must consider:
- Languages
- Tools

- Methods
- Processes

Maximizing the likelihood of success is a *question of balance*: Management must consider each of these aspects of a project in almost equal proportions.

LANGUAGES

The selection of which programming language to use in a given project is typically a binary issue, meaning that it is either a moot point or it is a hotly contested and almost religious one. In the first case, it may be a dead issue because some corporate or governmental mandate requires that it be a certain way. It may also be a dead issue because of the millstone of legacy code or legacy practices. (*"If COBOL was good enough for my grandfather, then it's good enough for me!"*) In either case, such unenlightened choices have some subtle and negative consequences. In particular, if a mandate is made for anything other than legitimate business reasons, then there can be no meaningful return on investment, and there will often be rebellion among the troops, who feel they are stuck with a dead language. Similarly, there may be good reasons for sticking with a legacy language, but there are rarely any good reasons for ignoring the evolution of that language. (Are you still using the same COBOL compilers from the 1960s?)

In the second case, underdeveloped organizations are often the battleground for extended language wars. "Should we use C++? What about Visual Basic? Or Smalltalk?" I'm not saying that such discussions are wrong, in general, but they are detrimental when they divide an organization along language lines and the team spends endless person-days arguing over the relative merits of one language versus the other. This is why I call such organizations underdeveloped: They become paralyzed, unable to move forward until all the data is in (which it rarely is). My advice in such situations is to just try something. Build something real with any one new language, and see how it fits your culture. Don't expect perfection, for no single language can meet all possible needs. The trick is to chose one that fits reasonably well for the scale of problem you are solving, and to chose one that gives you a good return on investment.

Where does scale fit into this discussion? I've seen more than a couple of projects fail because they tried to use something like Visual Basic to engineer a whole enterprise.[3] I've seen projects that automate some office process by using any of a number of application builders, then try to scale that experience up to the department or division or corporate level, only to fail in rather visible ways. At some level of complexity, raw, naked programming languages such as C++ and Smalltalk make a great deal of sense. By all means, use languages and frameworks that help you avoid writing new software, but don't stretch those languages beyond what they can meaningfully handle, without your developers having to resort to unnatural acts of programming.

So, as a matter of balance when it comes to language, my advice is simply to put a stake in the ground with regard to a selection, validate that selection in a pilot project, and if the results are good enough, then move forward, with few regrets.

TOOLS

The selection of tools for a project deserves equal treatment to the selection of language. Despite the latest advances in hardware, most of the development organizations I encounter are still woefully underdeveloped when it comes to the tools with which they arm their developers. A compiler, editor, and debugger are just *not* enough.

- *Analysis and design* tools are necessary to allow the team to discuss the problem and its implementation architecture at an appropriately abstract level.

- For projects of any meaningful scale, issues of *configuration management* kick in very quickly—this is something for which simple tools, rather than programmer convention, should be employed to handle the details.

---

[3] I'm not saying it can't be done. Exxon is a good existence proof of this. At issue is how hard is it to do so with any one given language. My experience is that it's very hard indeed, especially if you are concerned about the cost of ownership of that software. [Note that this was written prior to VB 4. See VB articles in chapter 7, Implementation.]

- *Testing* is typically under tooled. The most mature organizations I encounter have some form of automated regression testing that relieves the burden upon the individual developer, and furthermore serves as a stabilizing influence as a project unfolds.

- Other tools such as *browsers, intelligent debuggers,* and *metrics* tools all have a role to play as a project grows.

My advice is that given a tedious, repetitive development activity, I'd much rather buy or create a tool that does it for me, rather then spend precious developer hours having to do it by hand. Developers are a far more precious commodity than tools. Unfortunately, I do find some organizations have an easier time procuring new developers rather than necessary tools.

The dark side of tools is that underdeveloped organizations tend to find sort of a moral anchor in the form of some really cool tool. Perhaps finding some of their development efforts floundering, like a drowning man, they will grasp at whatever tool happens to float, only to find that faith in any one technical tool will indeed drag them down. Trying to apply a technical solution to a nontechnical problem always has a way of turning on you. The lesson here is to never let your project get intoxicated with any in-vogue commercial tool or trend. Be realistic about what your tools can and can't do for you.

Tools, then, are also a matter of balance: Consider what aspects of your entire development process can be automated, and by all means select some tools that fit. Don't seek perfection but seek simple tools that do some simple things very well.

METHODS

Underdeveloped organizations are also commonly the battleground for method wars. Studying which object-oriented method to employ is a good thing, but I've stepped into numerous companies where entire teams had spent literally months of time on this, independent of any software project. Such a situation represents a clear imbalance, because it attempts to force a technical decision in the absence of any real context within the organization.

With regard to methods, the real enemy is chaos, for most projects follow no identifiable method. In practice, that translates into developers rushing into coding with little regard for any overall design or understanding of what needs to be built. Mitigating those elements is ultimately the purpose of any object-oriented method, be it Booch, OMT, Objectory, Shlaer-Mellor, or any of a number of other mature methods. Again, it's a matter of balance. At least pick some method, any method, and fit it into your culture. Don't allow your method to be dominated by the act of coding, but don't let it overshadow implementation either. Ultimately, the production of real, concrete software is what every project is about.

PROCESS

When I speak of process, I mean it in a larger sense then just the technical process of crafting a software solution. This means a deliberate consideration of processes for testing, configuration management, change management, and reviews. Too many organizations fall into either one end or the other of a spectrum. At one end, they have no formal processes, but instead rely upon hiring lots of good people and letting them do what they do. This may make sense for a start-up project, but it is never a sustainable or repeatable practice. At the other end of the spectrum, the organization is dominated by a process czar, who dictates exactly what the software development process is to be. There are two fundamental problems with this. First, by the very nature of this position, a process czar is often isolated from the daily blocking-and-tackling of coding, and so is ignorant of all the pragmatic engineering decisions that color any real process. Second, no real project follows any one process. There will always be multiple processes going on at all times, and a reasonably complex project can be defined in a single-threaded process. This is why the Booch method defines both a macro and a micro process: The macro process focuses on activities on a time scale of weeks, months, or years, and the micro process focuses on activities on a time scale of days or weeks.

The lesson here is also one of balance: Be deliberate when considering the maturity of your organization's process. At the very least, do have and enforce some recognizable processes, but at same time, don't be foolishly rigid in their deployment.

There's a funny paradox that arises given this attitude. By way of foundation, let me state that I'm a believer in the work at the Software Engineering Institute regarding process maturity.[4] I view it as is a sign of maturity in our industry that we are beginning to model and quantify the way people build software. ISO 9000, as it applies to software, plays a similar role, in that it forces development organizations to actively consider how they do business. Now, here is the paradox: Successful projects tend to rate high on the SEI CMM; however, a high rating on the CMM does not necessarily imply success. The implications are simple. Process maturity should never be a goal in and of itself, but should be viewed as one visible sign of a healthy organization.

CONCLUSION

Software development remains hard. I don't expect it to get radically easier, mainly because there is a natural tendency for growth toward more complex applications. As a result, every industrial-strength organization needs all the help it can get. Maximizing likely success means striking a balance in the use of languages, tools, methods, and processes.

---

[4] Specifically, I'm referring to the SEI Capability Maturity Model (CMM), which defines several levels of process maturity. The Software Engineering Institute is a federally funded research and development center (FFRDC) sponsored by the U.S. Department of Defense and operated by Carnegie Mellon University. See *http://www.sei.cmu.edu.*

CHAPTER 2

THE BUSINESS OF OBJECT TECHNOLOGY

Clearly, software is becoming more and more strategic for many companies, but under what set of circumstances is the selection of an *OO* approach the right business choice? Grady has seen his share of successful and unsuccessful software projects and has addressed the business perspective of OO in the several articles included here:

- *The Software Landscape*[1] segregates the OO software market into broad categories. Here Grady explains the applicability of OO to each of these market segments.

- *Software as a Strategic Weapon*[2] discusses how software as a business tool is most successful when fulfilling a business vision. Not only is software essential to most businesses in the late twentieth century, but software that is consistent with business strategies can be used for competitive advantage.

- *Objectifying Information Technology*[3] contrasts client/server development within the context of object technology, and discusses observations about the adoption of object technology in information systems domains.

- The *Business Case for Class Libraries*[4] discusses investment for reuse and the market for reusable class libraries. Notice how the market has evolved since this article was published in 1993.

---

[1] Based on Booch, G. (1995). Coming of age in an object-oriented world. *IEEE Software 11*(6).

[2] Based on Booch, G. (1995). Software as a strategic weapon. *Object Magazine 4*(9).

[3] Based on Booch, G. (1993). Objectifying information technology. *Object Magazine 3*(3).

[4] Based on Booch, G. (1993). The business case for class libraries. *Object Magazine 3*(1).

- Finally, *The Microsoft Effect*[5] provides a critique of one of the world's largest software development organizations. Here, Grady discusses the relationship between business success and software development process maturity. In this article, Grady actually comes not to bury Microsoft, but to praise them, pointing out many issues that are, in fact, common to most development organizations.

Grady has also addressed "business topics" in *Object Solutions*. For example, in a section originally published as *The Business Case for Object-Oriented Projects*,[6] Grady addressed costs and returns that a team can expect while adopting object technology.

THE SOFTWARE LANDSCAPE

Before I am accused of adding to any smoke and noise about all things object oriented, let me first suggest a natural division in the kinds of software being created today, and then consider the role that object orientation plays in each.

Off-the-shelf software	Custom software
• Codifies some specific horizontal domain	• Architected along a vertical line of business
• Directed to a large market	• Typically involves the unique composition of many off-the-shelf components
• Eventually turns into a commodity	• Is inherently complex because of a lack of prior domain models

---

[5] Based on Booch, G. (1995). The Microsoft effect. *Object Magazine* 5(6).
[6] Booch, G. (1994). The business case for object-oriented projects. *Object Magazine* 4(6).

OFF-THE-SHELF SOFTWARE

Perhaps the largest and most central class of software includes all the various off-the-shelf components found in the industry. In this group we include operating systems and programming development environments (such as Microsoft Windows, Apple Macintosh, and all the various flavors of Unix, plus development tools such as Borland C++ and ParcPlace-Digitalk Smalltalk), personal productivity tools (including Microsoft Word, Lotus 1-2-3, and Lotus Notes), and many vertical domain-specific applications (such as Adobe Pagemaker for desktop publishing, Adobe Photoshop for imaging, Mathematica for scientific calculations, and Opcode Vision for orchestration). In terms of worldwide sales, off-the-shelf is likely the largest class of software. It is difficult (and probably unnecessary) to place an exact number on the size of this market, although most estimates would place it in the order of magnitude of tens of billions of dollars per year. I consider this group of software as most central, largely because its existence has launched entire industries and empires that collectively have made the business of computing fundamental to all tactical (but rarely spiritual) aspects of life.

Most instances of off-the-shelf software share at least three common characteristics:

- First, each tends to represent the codification of some aspect of a specific, reasonably well-defined problem domain. For example, Lotus 1-2-3 addresses the problem of financial modeling, Microsoft Windows NT attempts to addresses the issues of computing services in a complex, heterogeneous environment, and Powerbuilder focuses on the domain of user interface modeling in a client/server environment. Obviously, it is simply not economical to develop an off-the-shelf piece of software for a domain that we poorly understand.

- Second, most off-the-shelf software is driven to higher levels of sophistication primarily by market forces. If your potential market includes hundreds of thousands of users, competition will more likely lead you to invest the resources necessary to continually improve the value pile of your application. This is not feasible if your market has only a hundred or even a few dozen users.

13

- Third, over time, most broad, competitive off-the-shelf domains turn into a commodity market item. Consider, for example, the price wars and market posturing that have taken place in the arena of personal computer databases.

These three characteristics suggest a number of important consequences. In such software markets, the opportunity is tremendous, as is the risk. Any company wishing to tackle a particular vertical off-the-shelf domain must be prepared to make a significant investment, not just in software development costs, but also in marketing and ongoing support and maintenance. Indeed, in the steady state of this market, when the domain starts becoming saturated, companies that have survived and are still players will likely find that most of their revenues derive from upgrades, not from new customers. Getting a reasonable return on investment is further complicated by the combinatorial explosion of hardware/operating system/network choices, which requires vendors in this market to invest scarce marketing resources (to guess which combinations their customers want) and scarce technical resources (to make their applications work for each permutation), instead of advancing the software's functionality. Except for the biggest players—and even for them, this represents a significant drain of resources—most software development organizations are mere pawns in the hardware/operating system/network wars.

Enter object-oriented technology. If current trends continue, most of the world's next-generation operating systems will in *some* manner be object oriented: Consider, for example, Microsoft's Windows 95 and NeXT's NeXTSTEP. Most sophisticated user interfaces are already largely object oriented: Windows and the Macintosh have set the foundation for a whole generation of direct-manipulation idioms. Most canonical solutions to the problem of distributed data management are already object oriented: CORBA,[7] SOM,[8] COM,[9] and UNAS[10] are but four different object-oriented

---

[7] Common Object Request Broker Architecture, Object Management Group. See *http://www.omg.org*.

[8] System Object Model. See *http://www.software.ibm.com/objects/somobjects*.

[9] Component Object Model. See *http://www.microsoft.com/intdev/sdk/docs/com/comintro.htm*.

solutions to the same problem. Actually, these are only the more visible influences of object-oriented technology to the domain of off-the-shelf software. For a development organization that has to cope with various hardware/operating system/network combinations, object orientation has proven to be an effective approach to crafting architectures that are reasonably insensitive to the different permutations, or at the very least, are relatively easy to extend and adapt as requirements evolve.

From my experience, I've found that object-oriented technology continues to attract the interest of off-the-shelf software developers, largely because it addresses the economic problems of time-to-market, cost of software ownership, and resilience to change. Why does object-orientation help in these domains? Largely for the following reasons:

- The use of continuous integration creates opportunities to recognize risk early and make incremental corrections without destabilizing the entire development effort.

- An object-oriented model of a problem and its solution encourages the creation of a common vocabulary between the end users of a system and its developers, thus creating a shared understanding of the problem being solved.

- An object-oriented architecture provides a clear separation among disparate elements of a system, creating firewalls that prevent a snag in one part of the system from rending the fabric of the entire architecture.

CUSTOM SOFTWARE

The second, although not any less important, class of software I find encompasses what is commonly called *custom applications*. In this group I include mission-critical, enterprise-specific applications for a particular line of business, as well as truly embedded applications, such as software for home appliances, cars, and medical devices. For example, the computing systems that a retailer such as Walmart has, served to give them an advantage over less-automated competitors. Specialized financial systems make it possible for trading companies to create new derivatives in an already crowded,

---

[10] Universal Network Architecture Services. See *http:/www.rational.com/products*.

frantic market. In this group, I also include many technical applications, whose number of end users may be very small (i.e., one), yet to each such user they are essential. For example, custom software development is required for each new commercial aircraft, encompassing all of its aspects from flight-control systems, to ground-based maintenance equipment, to simulators, to in-flight entertainment systems. Similarly, each new public facility, such as the new Denver International Airport or the England/France Chunnel, requires a significant amount of custom software, without which the resource would be far less effective. An astronomer studying images from the Hubble space telescope may require custom software to examine patterns of emissions from distant stars.

Most instances of custom software share at least three common characteristics, each quite different than the properties of off-the-shelf software that I described earlier:

- First, *most custom software is generally architected along a given vertical line of business.* For this reason, we find companies that do nothing but craft then adapt frameworks for specific markets such as ship-board command and control systems or customer support services for public utilities. The requirements in these domains are often very ill-defined at first, although ultimately quite clear to the final user, unlike most off-the-shelf software. Furthermore, the shapes of the resulting architectures are quite different from domain to domain. For example, a custom financial application will generally be data-centric, whereas software for an autonomous people mover will often be event-driven. By contrast, most GUI-centric, off-the-shelf personal productivity software is message-driven.

- Second, *custom software is rarely fully custom, but more ofteninvolves gluing existing off-the-shelf components together in interesting ways.* For example, many banks and insurance companies—struggling under the sheer weight of ancient computing infrastructures—have found client/server computing as a way out of the past. Although off-the-shelf products for user interfaces, networking, and database management exist, each particular situation requires the development of some amount of custom software necessary to weave those pieces into the rules and culture of the particular business.

- Third, *developing custom software is honestly a really hard thing to do as compared to most off-the-shelf software, largely because of the unknown.* If I chose to write a new word processor, I can find lots of models of what works, what doesn't, and what customers want. If I chose to write the network management software that unites the services of my local cable company with banking, shopping, and entertainment services, I don't yet have any good and/or complete models to chose from. Furthermore, in such domains, the end users themselves most often don't have a clear picture of what they want or much less understand what is possible, and the mere presence of an automated solution changes the rules—and hence the demands—of its end users.

Consider the consequences of these characteristics of the custom software market... In this domain, software represents the *soul* of the system. Without a specifically tailored piece of software, a bank could not conduct business, the government could not process tax returns, a manufacturing company could not control its automated equipment, and an astrophysicist could not conduct an experiment. However, for each of these domains, software is a real burden, because it represents a necessary yet unavoidable resource. These businesses are not in business to write software, although in each case, each domain derives essential value from custom software.

Object-oriented technology has increasingly become an important factor in the world of custom software. For example, for a large publishing company that controls many smaller publishing houses (often inherited through acquisition or merger), it is quite sensible to craft a common, object-oriented framework for managing orders. This framework can then be adapted to each individual business, as they require slightly different business rules. For a trading company that lives and dies on the availability of custom software to handle new offerings, using object-oriented technology makes it far easier to adapt to rapidly changing market conditions. For a cable company that wants to offer innovative services that are yet undefined, object-oriented stuff offers a way to create a foundation that has value to customers immediately (so as to preempt the competition), yet that will not be impossible to change as consumers become more discriminating.

In short, I've found that object-oriented technology continues to attract the interest of custom software developers, because it addresses the economic issues of time-to-market, cost of software ownership, and resilience to change, exactly the same problems faced by developers of off-the-shelf software.

PROGRAMMING WITHOUT PROGRAMMING

Before I continue, let me state flatly that I do not view object-orientation as the universal solution to the ongoing imbalance between software supply and demand. Indeed, the wisest solution to this problem is to change the rules of engagement so that the problem disappears entirely. In Dr. Mary Shaw's terms, this means *programming without programming* (Shaw et al. 1996).

The problem of software supply and demand is not unlike what was faced by the telephone companies in their early days where, as the folklore goes, planners suggested that the number of operators required to manage the growing domestic telephone network would soon reach ridiculous levels. In short, everyone in the country would have to become an operator! Well, that's exactly what happened! In a sense, each telephone user is an operator, able to achieve some degree of end-user programming.

This analogy applies to certain, codifiable application domains. For example, every small business has its own financial model, yet unless there is compelling reason to do so, it's awfully foolish to spend the resources to develop a new piece of software that models only that business. Instead, it is far better to take an off-the-shelf spreadsheet application (that codifies an element of financial modeling) and create a model particular to that business. Sure, there is still programming involved, yet this end-user adaptation is done in the vocabulary of the problem domain, not in the realm of some distant implementation domain. Similarly, every user-centric application requires sophisticated windows and widgets. Unless the nature of the application demands it, it is far more sensible to use some sort of GUI-builder (which codifies a particular model of human-computer interaction) to paint the standard parts of the interface, then use custom software to glue those pieces together with the rest of the application. Again, this is an example of programming in the vocabulary of the problem domain.

This kind of programming without programming is not by any means a complete solution, for it does not address problems that lie outside the domain that has been codified. Furthermore, the problem of software supply and demand is not the only software problem our industry faces. Software quality, reliability, correctness, and the cost of ownership are but a few of the issues that will not go away, even though we may try to ignore or wish them away.

MATURITY AND ADOPTION

There are a number of signs of the growing maturity and acceptance of object-oriented technology. We are far beyond the point of early adopters, who will try just about anything new, simply because it is new. The technology has proven its value in a multitude of applications around the world. I have seen object-oriented languages and methods used successfully in such diverse problem domains as securities trading, medical electronics, enterprise-wide information management, air-traffic control, semiconductor manufacturing, interactive video gaming, telecommunications network management, and astronomical research. In fact, I can honestly say that in every industrialized country and in every conceivable application area, I have encountered some use of object-oriented technology. Object-oriented stuff is indisputably a part of the mainstream of computing. As such, it will form the foundation for the next generation of software architectures in numerous domains.

Presently, the vertical application domains for which I find object-oriented technology to have had the greatest penetration include aerospace, telecommunications, and financial services. I am beginning to see increasing use of the technology for general mission-critical MIS applications, suggesting that some of the less-conservative mainline businesses have gained enough confidence in early pilot projects to commit significant capital to object-oriented enterprise modeling. The transportation industries, health care, and entertainment industries (including computer gaming and special effects wizardry) are also emerging as significant domains touched by object-oriented technology.

In addition to the technical issues of time-to-market, cost, and resilience mentioned earlier, it appears that two business factors will continue to propel object-oriented technology into the mainstream of computing. First, object-oriented architectures help to encourage the creation of a line-of-business software organization. For example, software required for running public utilities is largely the same from city to city, although each individual utility is subtly different. This creates an opportunity for a company to craft a framework for public utility software, and achieve high leverage through selling and adapting the same framework over and over again. Object orientation helps technically by making such frameworks possible and practical, which in turn encourages a line-of-business orientation of the software development organization that creates such a framework. Second, the current push for business process reengineering encourages an object-oriented view of the world. As organizations continue to downsize while simultaneously being forced to play in an increasingly competitive global market, software becomes a more important strategic asset. As a business reengineers its processes, this scenario-oriented view of the enterprise's resources can readily and naturally be modeled in terms of objects.

There of course remain a number of interesting open issues for object-oriented technology as this century comes to a close. For example, the increasing demand for quality software—as manifest in standards such as ISO9000—requires even greater rigor in object-oriented methods. As more and more projects gain experience with object orientation, we will be better able to articulate these measures of goodness. On another front, the continuing reconciliation of an object-oriented view of the world with more traditional relational data models must continue. The reality is that the relational model embodies a certain attractive mathematical rigor, and has proven its worth in a number of domains; quite frankly, it is sufficiently pervasive to be entrenched. Emerging standards such as SQL3, which adds an object-oriented bent to SQL, are signs of progress in this area. Lastly, the exploration of patterns in object-oriented software appears to be a very promising spin on object orientation. The study of patterns, inspired by the work of Alexander, suggests a way to codify many of the common microarchitectures found in well-structured object-oriented systems.

Will object-oriented technology be a part of the mainstream of computing beyond the turn of the century? Undoubtedly, yes. Will some other software technology soon take its place? Possibly, for that is the nature of scientific progress, although there are as yet no clear signs of any other revolutionary advances in software that address the issues that object-orientation tries to confront. Will object-oriented stuff be sufficient to deliver the vision of technology found in *2001: A Space Odyssey*? Assuredly, no. However, it is the dream of such things that causes us to reach beyond what our current technology offers, and it is the pursuit of such visions that makes our modest contributions enjoyable.

SOFTWARE AS A STRATEGIC WEAPON

As I write this column [in mid-1995], the annual feeding frenzy called Comdex is winding down. Weighing in as the world's largest computer trade show, Comdex is a place where the small companies show up to sell their dreams and the big companies show up mainly just to posture against one another.

Comdex's size is equal perhaps only to the visions of computing that echo through its hallways. I find it particularly fascinating to read reports of who said what, because such statements often telegraph the intent of the major players. From Microsoft, Bill Gates spoke his usual story on the pervasiveness of computing. Visions of digital cash, software agents that roam the global networks, and automation of even the most mundane devices from phones to FAXes to household appliances, are not new ideas, but Gates brings to the table a view that ties all these disparate things together. From Intel, Andy Groves spoke his story on the integration of media in the personal computer. Again, the idea of combining text, graphics, video, speech, and sound is not new, but when it comes from the president of the company whose chips dominate the personal computing industry, you wonder what it means.

What it means to me personally is that the computing world does not lack for vision. Watch the ads on television from any of the various telephone companies, and you'll see their dreams for communications in the coming years. Read any of the computer trade magazines, and you'll soon overload just reading about the new alliances among players in the entertainment industry and financial industry with those in the computer world, and the hopes for pervasive automation that those alliances portend.

Now, I'm a great believer in always trying to reach for a vision just beyond one's grasp. However, there is a dark side to all this dreaming, and so I offer some pragmatic caution.

Talk to some of the programmers in the trenches of these various telephone companies, and you'll get a subtly different story than what their visionaries say. My experience is that most of the world's phone companies are drowning in a sea of software, weighed down by grossly complex systems that require tremendous care and feeding and that are flatly resistant to change. Most of the software development organizations in these companies find it hard enough just to keep up with current needs, much less spend the resources to chase their visions. Indeed, if the visions stopped, most of these teams would still be busy for many years, propelled by the sheer momentum of all the work they already have on their plates.

Talk to some of the programmers responsible for supporting the entertainment companies (and the financial companies with whom their leaders have aligned their companies). In most shops, you'll find a sort of controlled panic. They are *controlled*, because they are all professionals trying to do the right thing, and *in panic*, because both the stakes and the risks are high, leaving no room for failure.

My observation is that there are two dominant forces at play that drive the software industry to its visions: the *increased connectivity* of distributed computing systems and *greater user expectations* for better visualization of and access to information.

If software development were a perfectly understood craft, then chasing these visions would be a simple matter of programming. However, in the real world it is much, much harder than that, and no single technology—not even

OO stuff—will make the problem go away. To begin with, there is a natural inertia in every organization that governs how quickly it can absorb new technology. Convincing a well-entrenched COBOL shop to give up its mainframes is hard enough; bringing its programmers kicking and screaming into a brave new object-oriented world is something that does not happen overnight (and in certain cases, will not happen at all). Additionally, the frenzied pace of change in the industry adds significant noise to any team just trying to do its job. For organizations building distributed applications that span different platforms, simply keeping up with the stream of new operating system releases, the emerging distributed object managers, and the evolution of technology for persistence is horribly distracting. However, pragmatics dictate that the development team cannot stop change, and so has to make intelligent decisions in the face of limited information. Make the wrong decisions, and your project will eventually die a painful, lingering death; make the right decisions, and you'll be guaranteed to survive just long enough to have to make a new set of equally important decisions shortly.

While I'm on this path of preaching gloom, let me suggest that it's even worse than it sounds, because of the almost maniacal schedule pressure placed on many projects. Not surprisingly, different projects march to different beats, and so have different time horizons. Indeed, I've seen successful object-oriented efforts whose life cycles vary from several hours to several years. Consider the following spectrum of life cycles that I've encountered, as measured from project inception to delivery:

- *Less than a day* — sometimes found in the frantic world of financial services, where missing a trading window can mean millions of dollars in lost revenue.

- *A few weeks* — typical of exploratory development, such as when prototyping a larger effort or running experiments against a shifting source of data.

- *A few months* — often found in the steady state of a hyperproductive organization that's able to spawn new releases quickly from the base of a mature framework and that's driven by the desire to seize a window of opportunity in the marketplace. This time horizon is also common to some applications in the telephone business and in the entertainment industry, whose schedules are dictated by fickle consumer demand.

- *About one year* — perhaps the median duration for most object-oriented projects representing a fair capital investment.

- *A few years* — present in projects that affect an organization's entire line of business, and common in domains where hardware and software development must proceed in parallel. Projects of even longer duration exist, although I've seen very few of them succeed, at least as measured against the project's initial scope. In any case, geopolitical issues—not technical ones—tend to dominate, mainly because so much is at stake.

Note my observation about hyperproductive teams: in the steady state, they typically find a rhythm that permits them to be extremely nimble in the marketplace thus letting them drive their visions as opposed to being at the mercy of technological change. All of the hyperproductive projects I've encountered have the attitude that software is something that serves them, rather then they being a servant to its whims.

This is what I mean by viewing software as a strategic weapon. Banks are in the business of managing assets; software is just a business tool for responding to those needs. Libraries are in the business of facilitating access to information; software is just a means to that end. Manufacturing companies are in the business of creating hard goods from raw materials; software is a kind of soft goods that makes that process more efficient and hence more profitable.

This is the curious attitude that I find in all successful organizations: software is treated as an essential yet a secondary concern. Indeed, it is a mark of honor in hyperproductive organizations to write less software, not more, thereby leveraging the creative talents of its best people (who are ultimately the limiting factor in every organization). For such companies, software is a weapon because it furthers the business goals of the organization. Furthermore, it is strategic in nature because it can provide a competitive advantage.

This is why healthy organizations always seek to improve their ability to create software that meets their needs at a reasonable cost. This is why we see the drive to tools such as Microsoft's Visual Basic, Gupta's SQLWindows, Powersoft's Powerbuilder, and NeXT's development environment, all of which allow (as Dr. Mary Shaw calls it) "programming without programming."

It is my experience that while this genre of tools has its place, there are limits to the complexity each can handle. Where a domain is sufficiently understood and hence codifiable, then it is natural to find program generators. However, where the problem is not so well understood, then such application-specific tools fall flat.

This is why I'm jazzed by all this object-oriented stuff. Object-oriented technology seems especially suited to building application generators that codify specific domains. Object-oriented technology is also well-suited to building frameworks that capture the essence of less understood domains, by providing an enterprise model that embraces the vocabulary of the problem space, together with knobs and buttons in the framework that can be tweaked to adapt it to the particular needs of the problem at hand.

The suitability of object-oriented stuff to capturing the essence of a domain is what seems to be fueling the drive by many organizations to craft frameworks. Thus, we see companies such as Infinity with their class library for financial services. We see CelsiusTech with its framework for command-and-control systems. We see various telephone companies building frameworks for switching systems. And so it goes: the healthy organizations—recognizing that software is a major capital investment—seek to preserve that investment by building frameworks that allow them to evolve families of applications, each growing toward a vision that requires a deeper understanding and greater complexity.

The good news is that indeed object-oriented stuff works in this context, especially when an organization is dedicated to building frameworks that are approachable and that are designed to be much more than just a random sea of classes. The focus upon architecture and an incremental and iterative development process is central to all things object oriented, and furthermore is consistent with the business view of software as a strategic weapon.

Thus, those organizations that I see being successful in chasing their visions are those that are marked by three properties:

- They boldly attack the market by trying to dominate a particular line of business.

- They seek to efficiently leverage off their scarce development resources by architecting frameworks that codify those lines of business.

- They recognize that every good architecture requires an element of risk.

So, for those of you envious of distant visions for your business and equally confused by the hype of various software technologies, take heart, for you are not alone. Those organizations that I find making their way out of this morass are those that take a calm and deliberate approach to using object-oriented technology as a tool, along with whatever other technologies give them leverage and allow them to be nimble in the marketplace.

OBJECTIFYING INFORMATION TECHNOLOGY

What client/server computing is and is not is still a hotly debated topic. (Not unlike what is and what isn't object oriented.) Client/server computing can perhaps be best defined as:

- Whatever you want it to be, in order to explain to your management what you plan to do with all those personal computers that seem to be popping up in every department.

- Whatever the vendor currently pitching his/her products to you wants it to be.

A more serious definition suggests that client/server computing denotes "a decentralized architecture that enables end users to gain access to information transparently within a multivendor environment. Client/server applications couple a GUI to a server-based RDBMS."

Now, client/server computing is much more than a GUI plus an RDBMS, just as object-oriented programming is more than abstraction with inheritance, but the above definition does emphasize the importance of architecture. Indeed, the central strategic architectural decision that must be made in any client/server architecture is the division between the responsibilities of the client and the responsibilities of the server. Complicating matters intensely for the system builder is the fact that different vendors have thrown down different lines of demarcation. Standards along the client/server border are at best incomplete, sometimes in competition with one another, and unstable. All this disorder makes client/server software development quite a minefield, through which the architect must carefully step.

Some, including myself, would say that client/server computing is best carried out in the context of an object-oriented architecture. This is by no means a majority opinion, especially among some vendors who have built a large business around distinctly nonobject-oriented technology, and among companies who have a large capital investment in software. (Legacy code is like a dinosaur living in your office... no one in the organization may know exactly how it got there, but it's big, consumes mass quantities of resources to keep it alive, and demands attention. Some may suggest it should be killed, others may nurse it in the hopes that it will evolve to a higher life form.) This is not meant to be a value judgment: It's just a recognition that different players in the software industry see the object-oriented picture quite differently.

To some, OO stuff in the client/server world is only suited to crafting GUIs. An object-oriented user interface thus becomes synonymous with an object-oriented architecture. To others, stored procedures in a RDBMS are sufficiently expressive, such that true class-based schemas are unnecessary. Unfortunately, both of these views miss the point about object-orientation: architecting with classes and objects offers a way to unify our abstractions about a business' entire enterprise, in a manner that can lead to smaller and more facile architectures that can more easily be adapted as the rules of the business change.

EARLY ADOPTERS

Although critics may dismiss this last claim as yet more object-oriented hype, there is indeed considerable evidence that OO stuff really does make a difference. Consider for a moment, a few of the domains in which we have seen fielded systems constructed using object-oriented techniques.

Companies involved in trading systems seem to be among the earliest adopters of object-oriented technology in the MIS world. In retrospect, this is not surprising: software development turnaround in this business is often measured in weeks, not months, motivated largely by the rapidly changing international markets. As new financial instruments are devised in what is now a 24-hour-a-day marketplace, the company's software must adapt rapidly, or a window of opportunity may be lost forever to competition.

Inventory control is another functional MIS area where we have seen early use of OO stuff. Fielded systems exist for managing concessions at movie theaters, as well as inventory control at chains of gas and food convenience stores. At more than a few retail companies, we have encountered the use of object-oriented technology for their next generation of information systems. What seems to be the prime factor that has lead to these next-generation systems is the demand for more and relevant up-to-the-minute information about customers' tastes and buying patterns (which, perhaps unbelievably, change more often than faddish software development methods). A software system that can deliver such information becomes a key competitive asset to the company. Such an architecture cries out for client/server computing: Point of sale terminals feed database servers, from which GUI-oriented terminals are used to scrape out meaningful data. Such an architecture also cries out for object-oriented technology: The visual parts of such a system are obvious candidates for object orientation, but the requirement for distributed object processing naturally leads to an enterprise-wide view of the system in terms of common classes and common mechanisms whereby those classes collaborate. In this sense, OO stuff becomes the architectural glue that ties together off-the-shelf technologies, such as scanners and credit card readers (used at the point of sale), wireless notepads (used for taking inventory at the warehouse or in the store), and personal computers (tied to the network and used for analyzing buying trends).

Closely related to retail inventory management are the problems faced by the health care industry. Health management organizations (HMOs) are another domain for which we have seen only a few fielded object-oriented systems, although there are a fair number of such systems under development. The problems here are legion: Changing government regulations, coupled with customer demands for much simpler and more responsive services, together with the potential benefits and risks of keeping all of a patient's medical records available electronically, make this an area ripe for client/server computing and object-oriented technology. In the systems we have seen thus far in this domain, these two technologies provide the glue that ties together disparate off-the-shelf systems.

Utility companies are another group that seem to be migrating to object-oriented technology. Work at Brooklyn Union Gas serves as one well-documented and fielded use of OO stuff, and we are aware of a number of similar efforts throughout the country. The driving factor in this industry's software assets seems to be the demand for more and better customer services. Uncertainty with regard to the government's policies for taxing energy use has complicated the scene, but whatever the outcome, software becomes the vehicle whereby energy use can be tracked to individual households and businesses. Emerging technologies for online customer access to accounts, through various interactive cable services, is putting pressure upon this industry for more responsive services.

Banks and insurance companies—often stereotyped as extremely conservative when it comes to changing software development tools and processes—seem also to be opening up to object-oriented technology. Indeed, the economic pressure to move to client/server computing is often the door whereby object-oriented technology has entered such organizations. It's politically incorrect to mention any of these companies by name because, not surprisingly, most of them view their efforts as strategically very important, and hence offering a competitive advantage. Indeed, the growing demand for national banking services, together with deregulation, which has allowed banks to be much more than money changers, have together thrust software into a very central role in such businesses. Object-oriented technology has been the choice of a number of the players in this market, because it promises increased productivity and resilience.

We could fill many more pages with examples of traditional MIS organizations that are making a subtle but noticeable shift to OO stuff. A study conducted by CSC Index and reported in *Computerworld* (June 14, 1993) indicates that some 42% of the companies it surveyed were investigating object-oriented technology. In all fairness, this report also found only 6% were using object-oriented technology for production development. I was honestly taken aback by how low this number was in their survey—my intuition, based upon the engagements I've been involved with in North America, suggests that some 30-40% of traditional MIS organizations have some kind of production object-oriented system under development. But of course, you have to weigh my statistics just as you must weigh those from CSC Index or any other survey: Companies that are not interested in OO stuff tend not to contact me, so my data points are certainly biased. Still, although the relative numbers of MIS organizations using object-oriented technology may be a matter of statistical debate, there is no denying the large absolute numbers that are doing so.

COMMON MOTIVATIONS

An analysis of some of the early MIS adopters of object-oriented technology reveals some common threads. It seems that most have objectified their information technology organizations for one of two reasons: a desire for increased productivity and more predictable development costs and schedules, and a need for more responsive and adaptable services, motivated by demands from customers and competition. Those who are migrating to client/server architectures also seem to be migrating to object-oriented technology, and vice-versa.

Occasionally, we have seen a third reason. An organization adopts object-oriented technology because it looks fun and sexy and leading edge. Most such similarly-motivated organizations tend to fail because they have exactly the wrong attitude about the technology. Software development is not an end in and of itself to most companies, it is only a tool of the business.

BARRIERS TO ADOPTION

Why haven't 100% of MIS organizations adopted object-oriented technology already? There are the usual reasons for resistance of any new technology: uncertainty, lack of trained people, immature tools, a vested interest in the status quo—none of these are unique to object-oriented technology. However, there is one factor that is often cited and exists as a very real barrier to adoption, and that is the impedance match between the object model and relational databases. Let's consider this issue from a number of sides.

One company we encountered feared object-oriented programming because it wasn't as mathematically rigorous as relational database theory. It is certainly true that the relational model has a sound mathematical basis in set theory. However, it is also the case that pragmatics demands that real systems sometimes diverge from this pure model: Database designers regularly denormalize schemas for the sake of efficiency. In all fairness, object-oriented programming does indeed have a sound mathematical foundation: Classes are based upon the concept of abstract data types, which itself has a solid theoretical foundation.

We have also encountered MIS companies which suggest that object-orientation is unnecessary, because stored procedures are sufficient to couple data with behavior. We concur that they can be somewhat as expressive, except that stored procedures and triggers don't have the cohesiveness as does a class-based view of the world, and don't permit the sharing of behavior as is possible through inheritance. Stored procedures work if there are strong and consistent conventions for using them; a class-based view of the world helps to codify such conventions. Indeed, one of the reasons for SQL3, an object-oriented successor to SQL, is the desire for more rigorous abstractions.

A final form of resistance manifests itself in the fact that many MIS organizations have a large capital investment in RDBMS-related tools and people. The company's data is one of its key assets, and it is risky to rip out this foundational data while still trying to run the business from day to day. Of course, it is sometimes equally risky to do nothing, and suffer the effects of stagnation and data rot, whereby the company's databases become a millstone that inhibits nimbleness in the marketplace.

MIGRATION STRATEGIES

A conservative strategy, and one that I recommend often to such organizations, is to form a marriage between relational databases and the object model. The simplest solution is to form a thin object-oriented layer over the database; it is not difficult to devise mechanisms for translating navigation from object to object into appropriate SQL statements. In this manner, the object-oriented layer gives the illusion, albeit very incomplete, of an object-oriented database, while still preserving the relational database assets. This strategy then offers some degrees of freedom: Applications can continue to be developed using object-oriented techniques in the context of this framework, and the database can itself evolve, perhaps over time being replaced by an off-the-shelf object-oriented database, if the nature of the application is in fact suitable to that model.

A more aggressive solution populates this thin object-oriented layer with richer semantics. Specifically, we begin to codify the rules of the business in terms of the roles and responsibilities managed by various lattices of classes. This approach is more desirable, because it helps to centralized the enterprise's data together with its meaning and behavior.

This then is how client/server computing and object-oriented technology fit: A typical MIS system consists of a GUI, rules about the business, and its databases. At the very least, OO stuff provides a framework for the first two elements and, more aggressively, for the third as well. A client/server architecture draws a line somewhere across this framework, dividing the server and its clients. With object-oriented interfaces across this boundary, perhaps captured in the form of standard mechanisms such as the OMG's CORBA, the organization then has considerable degrees of freedom in drawing this client/server line independent of the GUI/rules/database decomposition. As the underlying technology changes, this separation of concerns becomes essential.

One clear sign that object-oriented technology is making inroads into traditional MIS shops is the fact that we are beginning to see pilot object-oriented projects at the level of city, county, and state governments, traditionally not among the first to embrace radical technology. The picture seems to be the same in Europe, and—perhaps surprisingly—within a number of Latin American countries.

The objectification of information technology appears to be here to stay, not because it happens to be the current fashion, but simply because it works.

THE BUSINESS CASE FOR CLASS LIBRARIES

Does there exist a sustainable market for reusable software components? The answer is a resounding ... *maybe*. Increased levels of reuse are often proclaimed as one inevitable consequence of object-oriented technology, and there is, in fact, anecdotal evidence to support this claim. We have encountered projects that report factors of reuse ranging anywhere from 20-80%, meaning that, in a given application, some 20-80% of the software in the delivered system did not have to be newly developed. It is significant that we have only rarely found comparable rates of reuse in projects not using object-oriented languages and methods. It is also significant that we have only seen higher levels of reuse in organizations for which reuse was vigorously encouraged by management.

Consider, for example, a reuse factor of 40%, a level within reach for a reasonably mature software organization developing a family of programs. In a modest application involving 500 classes, this translates into some 200 classes that do not have to be written, a savings of perhaps one person-year.

We could conclude, then, that from the demand side of the equation there is market for class libraries because there is compelling economic benefit. However, the supply side suggests a slightly different story.

Even in the presence of high demand (imaginary or real), there can exist a sustainable market only insofar as there can be a reasonable return on investment. Pundits may exclaim that reuse is "The Right Thing to Do," but unless a fair return is projected, commensurate with the development risk, no company will knowingly venture into the manufacturing of reusable software components. This is elementary economics, and the lesson applies equally to commercial purveyors of components and internal organizations responsible for project- or corporate-wide reuse.

BARRIERS PREVENTING RETURN

There are a number of barriers that tend to suppress the potential for return, but few of them are technical in nature. Software intended for reuse, by its very nature, demands a measure of quality, and this quality does not come without cost. It is relatively easy—but not free—to have locally high quality, as represented by individually crafted classes, so elegantly and cunningly fabricated they bring tears of joy to the user. However, the more elusive quality—and the more important for class libraries—is a kind of global quality represented by a conceptual integrity, a wholeness of the architecture. A poorly conceived architecture translates into a high learning curve for the user: Given a library consisting of even just a hundred or so classes, learning the idioms and mechanisms of that library is no easy feat, yet this knowledge is essential if the user is ever to successfully apply the library. A class library is much more than the direct sum of its individual classes.

Consider also an internally developed class library that provides a company with a significant competitive advantage in some application domain. For that company to choose to place that library on the open market, there must be overwhelming monetary benefit to justify the risk of losing the advantage that the library provides to the organization alone. Furthermore, supporting that library as a product is very different than simply using the library internally. "Productizing" a library directly adds to the cost of the library: documentation, support, and marketing are all elements that must be considered. Some of the best libraries, therefore, will never make it to the open market, but this is the right of a free market.

Secondary barriers for the commercial reuse marketplace include legal issues. Software liability for the class-library author lies within largely unexplored legal territory. Software copyright law, especially in certain Eastern European and Asian countries, is at best vague or nonexistent, and in the worst case, clearly biased against the software creator. Furthermore, because there are no standards for delivery of reusable software components in the presence of multiple operating system and hardware platforms, delivery of the source code is often required. This can mean large risks for the software manufacturer, who might make a significant development investment only to irretrievably lose that investment through piracy.

THE CURRENT MARKETPLACE

Evidence for these and other barriers to reuse is found in the fact that the marketplace for reusable software components is still very small. There currently exist a few pockets of activities, such as with domain-independent libraries, class libraries for certain GUIs, and a few application frameworks. Many of the latter frameworks are promoted by the vendors of the very operating system the libraries support. In these cases, the vendor rarely expects a significant direct return from the library itself, but instead pursues other motives: The existence of the library facilitates the development of applications that create demand for the operating system, where the real margins for the business exist.

In the case that there are a handful of vertical application-domain libraries on the market today, these same types of motives seem to apply: The companies that create such libraries hope to recoup their investment not solely by selling source code but rather by selling system-integration services as well. For a complex library in a limited vertical market, it is sometimes more profitable to ship human technical representatives with every major sale rather than try to document the library sufficiently so that it can be used as a shrink-wrapped product. Now, this is not necessarily a bad thing: There is still significant value to the eventual user of the library—the essential lesson is that the class library is only a means to an end (i.e., the development of applications), not an end in and of itself.

THE FUTURE MARKETPLACE

So, will a robust market of reusable software components ever emerge? Yes, but expect it to mature only for certain vertical domains, where the risks associated with entering the reuse market are within reason. Conventional wisdom expects a software market consisting of many vendors selling many common parts, much like the business of integrated circuits or building supplies. However, the hardware analogy is somewhat flawed. Reuse in these domains works only because there are well-established patterns and families of patterns: The 74xx family of integrated circuits is one such example of a mature family of hardware abstractions. In software, we have not yet sufficiently codified such patterns and so there is not yet the proper catalyst for class libraries. However, we are hopeful: In some vertical application domains, such as patient management, securities trading, and inventory control, some organizations are beginning to use object-oriented technology to codify the common abstractions. Ultimately, some of this effort will reach the open market in the form of class libraries, and for the organization that does it first and/or best, the market will provide great rewards.

[Since the publication of this article in 1993, the industry has seen the growing adoption of robust horizontal class libraries, commercially available vertical frameworks for the health care and financial services markets, and an exciting patterns movement. The work by Microsoft and others to create line-of-business object frameworks is helping to legitimize this market. Still, the economics issues described by Grady still apply: The open market for components is still limited. This is especially evident in the market for Java applets, which is still at the level of a cottage industry.]

THE MICROSOFT EFFECT

The International Conference on Software Engineering (ICSE) attracts a fascinating group of practitioners, theoreticians, and thought leaders, all focused on the challenges of building complex software-intensive systems. At this year's ICSE, one presentation in particular stood out. I'll spare you the details, but I can summarize this speaker's talk in three simple sound bites:

- The Microsoft software development process involves a number of well-defined practices, including testing buddies, automatic regression testing, and a rigidly-driven rhythm of releases.

- Microsoft is making piles of money.

- Therefore, the Microsoft software development process is not only good, it is downright superior and ought to be emulated.

It took a while to peel the audience off the ceiling after hearing this message! Indeed, some in the crowed were absolutely livid over the twisted logic in this message; the financial end does not necessarily justify the technical means. In the opinion of several in attendance, the Microsoft development process was not only not world-class, but it involved some practices that violated every maxim of modern software engineering. Furthermore, the case for a cause-and-effect relationship was not clear: Is it Microsoft's superior business acumen or its superior software development abilities that has made it successful?

Overwhelming business success can often mask systemic flaws in your development process. This is the Microsoft effect: As one writer suggests, "it appears that Microsoft's profitability has provided the cash needed to buy their way out of the development problems they have encountered."[11]

To be fair, I'm not singling out Microsoft for this criticism simply because I'm a Macintosh zealot. Rather, I can legitimately make this criticism against a number of large software development organizations. If I had a few billion dollars of cash in the bank, improving my software development process would be far down my list of things to do. However, let me make a basic observation: Most organizations cannot buy their way out of their development problems. Indeed, it's quite the opposite: Most software-intensive organizations eventually live or die based upon their ability to follow through with a sustainable and mature software development process. In fact, as software becomes a strategic weapon for more and more companies, what distinguishes one company from another in the same vertical domain is the functionality of their software that ultimately provides benefits to a targeted set of end users.

In their defense, Microsoft's development process does have a number of good elements. For example, in general, their approach to testing pairs up

---

[11] Crawford-Hines, S. (1995). Comments on Cusumano. *Software Engineering Notes 20*(3),24.

one tester for every developer. This practice forces accountability on the part of the developer, and permits the testing team to engage in the development process far earlier than otherwise. The practice of automatic regression testing is also a good one. Basically, Microsoft's approach is to throw a battery of automatic stress tests against every intermediate release. This not only frees people from the tedium of testing complex software, but it also provides an early warning to the team that their release is drifting away from a baseline of acceptable functionality. Lastly, Microsoft's practice of forcing closure on intermediate executable releases on a regular basis is in general a good one, and is in fact exactly the kind of rhythm that I find in all successful object-oriented projects. (Although, in my opinion, their usual rhythm is too fast. Forcing releases faster than one or two times a week encourages feature creep at the expense of architectural simplicity and conceptual integrity.)

THE ROUGH EDGES

However, there is a dark side to this story. The process of building shrink-wrapped software is not necessarily applicable to every other software domain. Furthermore, even with the good practices that I've described, there are a number of warning signs that Microsoft's development process has some rough edges. A few of these warning signs include:

- Software bloat

There is no denying that many Microsoft applications keep getting bigger and bigger with every release. Every time I update my copy of Word, for example, I find that it not only takes more disk space, but its execution footprint is bigger. The same is true with Windows 95. Clearly, each of these products has more (some say too many) features than the last release, but one has to question if this growth in functionality is commensurate with the growth in size. Often, the best applications are the ones that are conceptually simple.

Another clear warning sign:

- Schedule delays

The press has bled all over Microsoft for its delays in deploying Windows 95. Certainly, a major complicating factor is that Windows 95 has to work with an incredible number of diversely configured computers. However, one has to ask: What would it have meant to Microsoft's revenue stream to have had Windows 95 released on time and with complete functionality rather than the situation now, where it is late to market and incomplete?

There's one final warning sign worth mentioning:

- Excessive development and support staff

Very few organizations can afford to have almost one tester for every developer, as many of Microsoft's main-line product teams seem to have. Not only is this a questionable practice in terms of overhead, but one also has to wonder how this slows down the individual developer, who might be better served by directed mentoring and focused walkthroughs. Similarly, there are signs that Microsoft's customer support staff is downright huge. Often, it's easier and quicker to expand your customer support organization than it is to get your development team to build simple software for complex applications. Not only is the overhead of a massive customer support organization costly, it's the mark of an unhealthy project that produces software that is hard to use.

MEASURING SUCCESS

If we say we want to conduct a successful software project, we must come to grips with what we mean by "successful." Only then can we establish practices that yield success. Finding a successful organization (by whatever measure) and then declaring its practices as good by implication is indeed flawed reasoning. Some of these practices may by good, as I've explained, but current success may mask all sorts of systemic evils in the development process that may not yield sustainable success.

How do I measure the success of a software project? I've two answers.

- First, the economic answer is that a successful project is one that makes piles of money.

- Second, there's the social answer: A successful project is one whose products delight and provide real value to the end user and along the way delight and provide real value to the people who build the software in the first place.

If your organization can do both, then you are working for a rare institution, indeed. It's easy to optimize for the economic answer, yet often this happens at the expense of the social answer, especially with regard to the full lives of the members of the development team. It's also easy to optimize for the social answer, only to find yourself driven out of business by more ruthless competitors.

In short, success is neither completely a business nor a technical issue—it's a balanced combination of both. What attracts me to the object-oriented paradigm is that well-structured object-oriented systems are resilient, which makes it possible to grow them as the needs of the business change, yet still preserve a stable system that over time can evolve to become simpler in form even as the problem domain grows in complexity.

CHAPTER 3

PROCESS AND PRODUCTS

In order to successfully execute a software development method, one must not only understand its notation and semantics but also how to develop models and software in the context of a sound engineering process. Regardless of whether a process is defined informally or with an exacting set of prescriptions, it must produce results in terms of a notation, consistent with its semantics.

In his 1993 book *Object-Oriented Analysis and Design with Applications*, Grady defined the macro and micro processes in fairly abstract terms. Since then, Grady has added new material on process issues, which remains consistent with this macro/micro world view.

With his focus on pragmatic issues, Grady's concentration has been to help settle the wars over notation and semantics. Still, the industry is left with widely varying opinions on process. In his words, "The object-oriented method wars regarding notation are largely over, but long live the process wars!" There are factors that merit the continuation of the process wars. For example:

- The very nature of software development and implementation keeps changing. Consider the emergence of Java and COM[1] and their impact on design and implementation.

- There can be many processes that achieve the same goal. The choice of which process is optimal will depend on many factors, for example, problem domain, culture, expertise, and the degree of novelty in the project. Defining a process framework wherein many varying instantiations of it can be accommodated remains an elusive goal.

Several of our colleagues at Rational Software Corporation are currently focused on process issues. Rational's philosophy of software

---

[1] Component Object Model.

development can best be summarized as "use-case driven, architecture-centric, and iterative and incremental." In short, the concept is to utilize use cases and scenarios to drive each development iteration while consciously refining the architecture, which among other things is concerned about the intelligent placement of responsibilities within a system. Iterations are defined with the express intent of satisfying requirements while mitigating project risk. This approach is a natural merger of philosophies from Rational and Objectory, which was acquired by Rational in 1995. Although the UML is intentionally silent on process, Grady, Jim Rumbaugh, and Ivar Jacobson have been vigilant to assure it will support the above-described process.

Our experience shows that this philosophy steers projects in the right direction and it is being endorsed through successful application. Still, don't hold your breath for an industry agreement on process any time soon. When I pressed Grady to summarize how he felt about the future of process, he told me the following story:

> Gandhi was apparently asked the question, "What do you think about Western civilization?" He answered, "It would be a good thing."

Then he answered my question, "What do you think about process?" with the same sort of response, "It's a good idea."

We include two articles on process in this chapter.

- *The Macro Process*[2] articulates the key points of the Booch macro process. Here, Grady discusses how the industry has diverse schools of thought on which techniques should drive a design. Grady praises the merits of a scenario-driven, iterative, and incremental process and discusses how this approach establishes a healthy rhythm for the team.

- To really know how well a process is working and how it can be improved, its results must be measured. In the second article, Grady

---

[2] Based on Booch, G. (1994). The macro process of object-oriented software development. *Report on Object Analysis & Design* vol 1(4).

describes *Measures of Goodness*,[3] which should be applied to a project, in context of the macro process.

Grady has also authored other articles describing the necessary artifacts of a successful OO project, including *Documenting Object-Oriented Systems*, which was incorporated into *Object Solutions*.[4]

THE MACRO PROCESS

I usually allow myself only one outrageous statement per column. Since I'm likely to get lots of e-mail on this one, let me get it out of the way first:

> *The object-oriented method wars regarding notation are largely over, but long live the process wars!*

Let me explain. If you ignore all of the cosmetic issues—which are to some degree a matter of personal taste—there seems be a remarkable consensus in what successful object-oriented projects use to model the behavior of their systems, the shape of their architectures, and the form of their implementations.

MODELING
In light of what many real projects use, I offer the following recommendations:

- **Scenarios are good.** They are essential for expressing the behavior of a system. Individual scenarios help visualize the threads of action that connect certain clusters of classes or classes in time. Groups of scenarios form a web that collectively denote the behavior of a system or the behavior of a major subsystem.

---

[3] Based on Booch, G. (1994). Measures of goodness. *Report on Object Analysis & Design 1*(2).

[4] Booch, G. (1995). Documenting object-oriented systems. *Object Magazine 5*(2).

- *Roles and responsibilities are good.* At some level of abstraction, the semantics of individual classes and objects is best expressed in terms of their roles and responsibilities. A major activity of the development team is the intelligent distribution of responsibilities across a system, so as to maximize flexibility and minimize complexity (two competing forces).

- *Class models are good.* Often expressed in some variant of class diagrams, these models are essential for showing the static semantics of enterprise models. These models also address the issue of scale in object-oriented systems, by allowing the visualization of structures that are larger than individual classes.

- *Collaborations are good.* Collaborations of classes and objects—typically expressed in some variant of object diagrams or interaction diagrams—are essential for visualizing the patterns within an architecture.[5]

- *In some domains, state machines are good.* For example, in reactive real-time systems, there are few better alternatives for expressing the dynamic semantics of classes and objects in the face of outside events.

I don't mean to overly simplify the dedicated efforts of any of my fellow methodologists, but I'm frankly amazed at a rapidly growing consensus in the core of fundamental semantic elements for the object-oriented analysis and design of real projects. Notation is also converging. Even as short as a couple of years ago, such a consensus was not even close to forming. However, now this consensus is becoming manifest in the evolution of second-generation object-oriented methods.

APPROACHES TO PROCESS

Alas, I cannot make the same positive statement with regard to process: there exists considerable diversity in thought over how the object-oriented project should conduct its business. To that end, I roughly divide the object-oriented

---

[5] [The UML terms are collaboration and sequence diagrams, respectively. These diagrams have gone through a number of name changes in the industry over the years, perhaps indicating some maturing process.]

world into five somewhat overlapping schools of philosophy regarding process:

- The *anarchists*, who largely ignore process and prefer to be left alone with their computers.

- The *behaviorists*, whose focus is upon identifying and then evolving roles and responsibilities.

- The *storyboarders*, who see the world in terms of scenarios.

- The *information modelers*, who focus on data and treat behavior as secondary.

- The *architects*, who focus upon frameworks (both building and using them).

My thoughts regarding process have indeed undergone a considerable evolution over the past 12 years.[6] Process is a hard thing, because it is a management issue that requires the reconciliation of two very difficult and opposing forces. First, there is the *tension between formality and informality*. Ultra-formal projects require so much ceremony that it stifles all creativity. Ultra-informal projects are chaotic, and hence unpredictable and unsustainable. Second, there is the problem of *conflicting time horizons*. Individual developers have a time horizon of a few hours to a few days or weeks. Projects as a whole have a time horizon of a few months to a few years.

After working with lots of object-oriented projects over the years—seeing some fail and many succeed—I'm finally at peace with how to reconcile these tensions. Simply stated, the answer appears to lie in distinguishing the macro and micro elements of the development process. The macro process is closely related to the traditional waterfall life cycle, and serves as the controlling framework for the micro process. The macro process is the primary concern of the software management team, whose time horizon is typically measured in weeks, months, and—for truly massive undertakings—years.

---

[6] Yes, 12 years [when this article was written in 1994]. My first paper on object-oriented design was published in 1982. Today, I consider myself an architect with deep influences coming from the schools of behavior and storyboarding.

The micro process is more closely related to the spiral model of development, and serves as the framework for an iterative and incremental approach to development. The micro process is the primary concern of the individual developer or a small group of developers, whose time horizon is typically measured in weeks, days, and—for really rapid development efforts—hours.

THE MACRO PROCESS

Let me focus upon the macro process, because it affects the entire flow of the object-oriented project.

Every healthy software project I've encountered has a natural rhythm whose beat is sounded by a steady and deliberate forward motion toward the delivery of a meaningful product at a reasonably-defined point in time. Even in the presence of a crisis, such as the discovery of an unexpected requirement or the failure of some technology, the healthy team does not panic. Rather, it is this steady rhythm that helps keep the project focused on its ultimate goal and gives the team its resilience to roll with the punches.

I've seen my share of unhealthy projects, and they tend to lack rhythm. The slightest crisis throws such a project out of whack. The mere mention of risks incites panic, manifested by its managers focusing on political games, its analysts paralyzed by details, and its developers burying themselves in their technology instead of focusing themselves on finding constructive solutions. To use an analogy, if the healthy software project is like a well-oiled, smoothly running machine, then the unhealthy one is like a broken-down engine, running in fits and starts, and belching out a lot of heat and smoke as it clanks along the way.

One important habit that distinguishes healthy projects from these unhealthy ones is the use of an iterative and incremental software development life cycle. An *iterative* process is one that involves the successive refinement of a system's architecture, from which we apply the experience and results of each major release to the next iteration of analysis and design. Each iteration of analysis/design/evolution is repeated several times over the object-oriented architecture. The process is *incremental* in the sense that each pass through an analysis/design/evolution cycle leads us to gradually refine our strategic and tactical decisions, extend our scope from an initially skeletal architecture, and ultimately lead to the final, deliverable software product. The work of preceding iterations is not discarded or redone, but rather is corrected and augmented. The process is also incremental at a finer level of granularity, that is, in the way each iteration is internally organized, as in a succession of builds.

This iterative and incremental process is also one that is risk-driven, meaning that for each evolutionary cycle, management directs the project's resources in such as way as to mitigate the project's highest risks, thus driving each evolution closer to a final, meaningful solution.

This is indeed the rhythm of all successful object-oriented projects. This is also the focus of the macro process, whose time horizon spans the entire software development life cycle, and whose activities serve as the central focus of management's attention and control. The rhythm of the macro process can be summarized in the following two practices:

- The macro process of the object-oriented project should comprise the successive refinement of the system's architecture.

- The activities leading up to every evolutionary release in the macro process should be risk-driven: First assess the project's highest risks, and then direct the project's resources in such as way as to mitigate those risks.

Now, I'm always trepidatious when explaining the macro process of object-oriented development. Some naive organizations, once understanding its phases and activities, will conclude that "*if I do x first, and then y, and then z, just as he told me, then I'll consistently deliver my perfectly maintainable and adaptable products on time and on schedule.*" Nothing could be further from the truth.

Successful software development is hard work, and no amount of ceremony will make that problem go away. At the other end of the spectrum are those organizations that reject any hint of ceremony, and so seek object nirvana from the perfect tool, the perfect language, or the most lightweight process. This leads to the magical software development life cycle wonderfully satirized by Orr and called the *One Minute Methodology*. As Orr wryly observes, the secret of the One Minute Methodology is simply that "*it's not important that you have real information, it's just important that you feel like you do* (Orr 1994, 35)."

Orr rightfully goes on to say that "*the truth is, building systems that are able to respond quickly to management needs takes a long time. Nobody wants to hear that...You can build good systems, and you can build them quickly, but you can't build them without skillful planning and solid requirements definition* (Orr 1994, 51)."

Skillful planning is what the macro process is all about. If there is a secret to this process, it's best summarized by the following practice:

> In the context of continuously integrating a system's architecture, establish a project's rhythm by driving to closure certain artifacts at regular intervals; these deliverables serve as tangible milestones through which management can measure the project and then meaningfully exert its control.

There are three important elements to this practice:

First, the macro process of object-oriented development is one of continuous integration. Rather than setting aside a single period of formal system integration toward the end of the life cycle, the object-oriented life cycle tends to integrate the parts of its software (and possibly hardware) at more regular intervals. This practice thus spreads the integration risk more evenly throughout the life cycle rather than back-loading the development process, where there is less room to maneuver if things go wrong.

Second, at regular intervals, the process of continuous integration yields executable releases that grow in functionality at every release. The delivery of these and other artifacts serve as milestone in the macro process (Jones 1994). In my experience, the most important such concrete deliverables include initial proof of concept prototypes, scenarios, the system's architecture, various incremental releases, and a punch list (for maintenance). Notice, by the way, that the refinement of a system's object-oriented architecture weaves a common thread through the macro process. This is indeed why I focus so much on the importance and meaning of architecture.

Finally, it is through these milestones that management can measure progress and quality, and hence anticipate, identify, and then actively attack risks on an ongoing basis. Management cannot control those things it cannot see. If risks are to be mitigated, then they must be explicitly sought out. Constantly reacting to risks as they reveal themselves is a recipe for disaster, because it destroys the rhythm of a project.

Why is the rhythm of the macro process so important? There are three key reasons:

- Iterative and incremental releases serve as a forcing function that drives the development team to closure at regular intervals.

- As problems arise—and they will—management can better schedule a suitable response and fold these activities into future iterations, rather than completely disrupt ongoing production.

- A rhythmic development process allows a project's supporting elements (including, testers, writers, toolsmiths, and domain experts) to better schedule their work.

This is what a mature development process is all about. The first step toward process maturity is to define a project's rhythm. Once this rhythm is established, then and only then can the project work to keep improving the beat.

If you happen to say, "But this is all just common-sense project management," you are somewhat correct. There is nothing radically new here. However, in the presence of object-oriented technology, there is one very different thing: Rather than discretely analyzing, then designing, then implementing a system from the top down, the object-oriented process tends to go from the inside out. In other words, we start with what we know, devise a skeletal object-oriented architecture, study the problem some more, improve upon our architecture, and so on, until we reach a solution that satisfies our project's essential minimal characteristics.

Thus, what Parnas observes is so true: *No real project of any substance flows top-down from a statement of requirements to a perfectly wonderful implementation.*[7] Rather, all real processes are both cyclic and opportunistic:

cyclic in the sense that they require iteration, and opportunistic in the sense that it is impossible to know *a priori* everything there is to know, and hence projects must react to things they discover along the way. However, Parnas also observes that it is important that the development process appear as if it's top-down—and that's the role of the macro process of object-oriented development.

As I see it, the major phases of the object-oriented macro process include:

- **Conceptualization** — Establish core requirements.

- **Analysis** — Develop a model of the system's desired behavior.

- **Design** — Create an architecture for the implementation.

- **Evolution** — Evolve the implementation through successive refinement.

- **Maintenance** — Manage post-delivery evolution.

Figure 1 provides an illustration of this process.[8,9]

---

[7] Parnas, D. & Clements, P. (1986). A rational design process: How and why to fake it. *IEEE Transactions on Software Engineering, SE-12*(2).

[8] We use a state-transition diagram here to represent the phases, or states, of the macro process.

[9] [Rational Software's current OO method training advocates four phases: *Inception, Elaboration, Construction,* and *Transition.* The activities of analysis and design continue throughout the development. These phases constitute a *management perspective* of a project, whereas the series of iterations constitute the *technical perspective* of the project's process.]

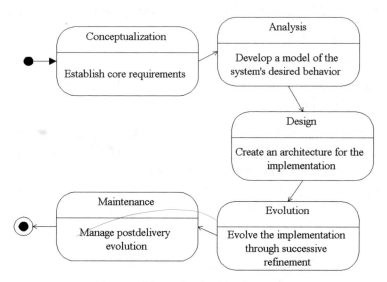

Figure 1. The macro development process.

Realize that the macro process is not like the strict, traditional waterfall approach to development. Rather, the macro process is explicitly iterative and incremental, and so is more closely related to Barry Boehm's seminal work on the spiral model.[10]

To further help you build a conceptual model of the macro process, let me describe it in broad strokes in another way, namely, in terms of the major activities in each phase:

- **Conceptualization** — Bracket the project's risks by building a proof of concept.

- **Analysis** — Develop a common vocabulary and a common understanding of the system's desired behavior by exploring scenarios with end users and domain experts.

---

[10] Boehm, B. (1986). A spiral model of software development and enhancement. *Software Engineering Notes, 11*(4).

- **Design** — Establish a skeleton for the solution and lay down tactical policies for implementation by crafting the system's architecture.

- **Evolution** — Refine the architecture; this phase typically requires further analysis and design.

- **Maintenance** — Continue the system's evolution in the face of newly-defined requirements.

One final way to think about the macro process is in terms of how its products unfold over time. In Figure 2, I've taken the five of the most important reusable artifacts as described by Jones, and plotted their development against the major phases of the macro process. The darker the band, the more focus being spent on that artifact.[11]

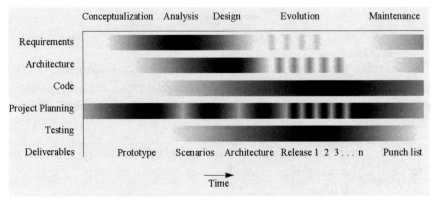

Figure 2. The rhythm of the macro process.

This illustrates the rhythm of the macro process. Thus, an understanding of a system's requirements evolves during analysis, and this understanding is revisited at each iteration. Similarly, a system's architecture begins to be formulated during the later phases of analysis, is made reasonably stable during design, and then is also refined in each iteration. Code artifacts grow steadily over the life cycle, with discrete jumps in code completeness at each

---

[11] Please note that the time axis in this figure is not to scale. Each of the phases of the macro process really take up a different amount of time, with evolution typically the longest phase.

iteration. Not surprisingly, testing tracks these code artifacts fairly closely. Finally, project planning hardly ever gets a break, for it must lead every other activity.

I must emphasize that every project is unique, and hence management must establish the right level of formality in its use of the macro process. For exploratory applications developed by a tightly knit team of highly experienced developers, too much formality will stifle innovation; for very complex projects developed by a large team of developers who are not co-located, too little formality will lead to chaos.

To reach a higher level of process maturity, each phase of a software development process must be described in terms of its
- Purpose
- Products
- Activities
- Agents
- Milestones and measures

CONCLUSION

The macro process provides meaningful management perspective for a project, focusing the team on its principal tasks, while recognizing that we cannot provide a cookbook generic enough for most projects. The successful projects I have seen have struck a healthy balance between process and results. To this end, the macro process is only part prescription (use-case driven, architecture-centric, and iterative and incremental), and therefore allows the team flexibility in how the products must line up against the process. There is growing industry agreement on the types of ingredients and qualities of our products, but not the exact recipe to produce them. Rightly so.

MEASURES OF GOODNESS

One of the signs of a mature software development organization is its use of certain reasonable and quantifiable measures of product and process. Such measures, if properly applied, can give management important insights into the health of a project. The most mature organizations are able to use these measures to make mid-course corrections in individual projects and in the company's software development activity as a whole.

The important phrase here is "reasonable and quantifiable"—*reasonable* in the sense of measuring those true properties of a system that are indicative of its quality, and *quantifiable* in the sense of being something that can be calculated with minimal pain. Thus, I'm not talking about certain apocryphal measures that even the most chaotic development organizations apply. For example, if your developers run screaming into the night, this is usually a sign of a project in crisis. Measuring the rate at which pizza boxes accumulate outside certain programmer's cubicles may appear to have some correlation with rate of progress, but even that is not a very reliable measure. (I am personally engaged in a highly scientific, international study requiring massive quantities of hairy mathematics to either validate or disprove this hypothesis. My belief is that pizza thickness and choice of toppings have some bearing. I assure you that through my selfless efforts, I will get to the bottom of this issue.)

Alas, reality is that not many real software projects in industry measure what they do. While in Europe recently, I asked a project manager at a large telecommunications company what metrics he applied to measure the health of his large, mission-critical network services application. He mumbled some answer about measuring the size and shape of inheritance lattices... but then admitted that there was really no formal metrics plan in place, other than gathering information about software defects. Rather, it seemed that he measured the health of his project informally, largely by observing the level of stress his developers were under at any point in time. This is a good way to tell if a project is already in crisis, but it is a singularly lousy way to predict a crisis. If your developers are under unnatural stress, then it's already too late.

Witness, for example, the debacle at the Denver International Airport. As I write this column [in mid-1994], the opening of this airport has been delayed indefinitely, at the cost of about one million dollars a day. The reason for the day-for-day slip: software and hardware problems in its automated baggage handling system. There were a number of obvious predictors of an impending software crisis, yet the real systemic problems were not uncovered until system testing, a point in time terribly late in the development cycle. No amount of heroic programming efforts are sufficient to rescue such a project in crisis, largely because its problems represent fundamentally wrong architectural decisions. This is why measuring certain architectural properties throughout the software development life cycle is so critical.

Yet, if standard industry practice is to not measure certain attributes of a project, then one might conclude that metrics are not all that important after all. Wrong. If you want to have a sustainable business, be it crafting software or crafting automobiles, you have to measure what you are doing, so that you can over time optimize your organization's development process. Why then do many projects reject measuring their products or process? The usual answer is that such numbers-gathering is viewed as overhead, and therefore irrelevant to the primary activity of the organization, namely, pumping out software. Such an attitude contains a tiny bit of truth, but then twists it in the wrong way. Measuring attributes of a product does not contribute to its raw generation, but it does help you in building a quality product and a quality organization.

Occasionally, I see projects that go to the other extreme, wherein they measure everything in sight, such as microscopic measures of member function complexity, frequency of certain language features, or—dare I mention it—amount of reuse. Focusing on low-level, language-oriented measures is typically misguided, because they measure the wrong things. While it might be intellectually interesting to know the average number of selections in all case statements, such measures have no relevance to the overall health or quality of a project. In short, if you focus only upon local measures of goodness, then you typically become blinded to the more important global characteristics of a system.

The issue of measuring reuse is a similar problem, although a bit more religious in nature. On the one hand, increased reuse is one of the much-touted advantages of all things object oriented. On the other hand, measuring reuse even at the class level is hard to track, and just assuming that you can measure it well, optimizing for the reuse of individual classes is often the wrong thing to do. There is far more leverage to be gained in reusing architectural artifacts that are bigger than classes. In short, if you define quantifiable measures of your product and process, you must be careful to select the right ones, because once you institutionalize it, every organization will tend to direct its activities to optimize these numbers at the expense of all other properties.

Why then measure at all? The first reason is that every project needs some basic predictors of project health. Knowing the size and basic shape of a system under development is essential in measuring where you are and how far you have to go. Certain measures of stability, as I'll discuss in more detail later, are critical predictors of a project in potential crisis. The second reason is that every project needs some measure of quality, so that hard business decisions can be made intelligently. Is my application ready for prime time? Measuring test coverage and defect discovery rates help give informed answers. What will be the cost of responding to particular changes in requirements? Knowing something precise about the shape of an architecture helps give an informed answer. Given limited resources, how should I direct my formal reviews? Understanding relative class complexity helps use our scarce time resources effectively.

One of forces that led me to evolve the second-generation Booch method was a desire to move object-oriented projects higher up the food chain in the SEI levels of process maturity. The demands of ISO9000 create a similar driving force. Both the SEI levels and the ISO9000 program seek to aid in the creation of predictable and quality software, and an essential element of both is the ability to measure a project's products and process. Thus, it is a sign of a mature software development method to define reasonable and quantifiable measures.

The bad news is that traditional metrics, such as measures of functional coupling, cohesion and complexity, just don't make much sense in the context of object-oriented architectures. The good news is that specific object-oriented measures of goodness have begun to surface and some of these appear to be useful predictors of a project's health. It is these kinds of measures that are a fundamental part of the Booch Method.

I will be the first to admit that I am not a guru in the area of software metrics, and so I have built upon the work of those who are. The value I've added is to show how these metrics fit into the object-oriented software development life cycle. To that end, my work has been influenced from four main sources. First, there is the work of Chidamber and Kemerer at the MIT Sloan School of Management, who have proposed a set of fairly tactical object-oriented measures. Second, there is the work of Tom McCabe, a pioneer in metrics, who has recently proposed a number of object-oriented-specific metrics very much in the same spirit as Chidamber and Kemerer's. Third, there is the work of various quality-assurance experts, including Robert Grady, Schulmeyer and McManus, and Jim Walsh. Fourth, there is the experience from a variety of projects with which I've been involved, which has sensitized me to the social aspects of instituting a metrics policy. An excellent published source for metrics is Mark Lorenz and Jeff Kidd's *Object-Oriented Software Metrics* (Lorenz & Kidd 1994*)*.

When I'm judging a product and process, I prefer to use the term "measures of goodness" rather than the sometimes more emotionally laden term "metrics," because I mean to cover those properties that span all dimensions of the system, some subjective and others brutally objective. To that end, I distinguish between strategic and tactical measures of a system. A strategic decision is one that has implications for the system's entire architecture, such as the choice to use a client/server architecture. Similarly, a strategic measure is one that measures the goodness of properties that relate to the health of a system's architecture. For example, observing the rate at which certain class categories change is usually a good predictor of stability and risk. (In a client/server architecture, this may point out areas of contention in the system where the client/server boundary has not been well-established.) In contrast, a tactical decision is one that has relatively local implications, such as the choice of a particular inheritance lattice or the choice of protocol for a specific class. A tactical measure seeks to judge the goodness of all such tactical decisions as applied across the system. This approach—observing local properties applied globally—has important implications for driving a project's consistency and integrity at the level of the individual unit of decomposition, namely, the class.

The Booch method employs several general kinds of measures. First, there are measures of *complexity*, such as measuring the number of classes in a system. Second, there are measures of *shape*, such as measuring the height and width of inheritance lattices. Third, there are measures of *risk*, such as measuring the stability of certain key interfaces. Lastly, there are measures of *defects*, such as the traditional defect discovery rate and defect density. It is important to note that there is a time and a place for each of these measures in the life cycle. Measure certain properties too early, and you will get misleading information. Measure certain properties too late, and, well, it will be too late to do anything about it, short of unwinding earlier decisions. To that end, the Booch method ties certain measures of goodness to various phases in the life cycle. This of course is not gospel: every project must tune these recommendations to their own culture. However, there are particular orderings that have worked well in a number of applications.

COMPLEXITY

From the perspective of management, the macro process represents the main focus for exerting control over a project. For each phase of the macro process, there are a number of complexity measures that are useful predictors of health.

During *conceptualization*, the primary product is an executable prototype that serves as a proof of concept. Unrestrained innovation is the hallmark of this phase, so most of its internal activities are left best unmeasured. What can and must be measured is the *time-to-completion* of this early prototype (this helps calibrate the development team and the project risk) and the *coverage* of this early prototype (this helps calibrate the level of future effort expected). Admittedly, these are subjective measures, but nonetheless they are reasonable, because they help in identifying areas of future risk.

During *analysis*, the primary product is a model of the system's desired behavior. In general, this means capturing the semantics of a system's behavior in a series of use cases, generated through the activity of discovery involving domain experts and a few key developers. With these more tangible products, it is possible to make more objective measurements. As a measure of process, I use the rule of thumb that development can proceed once about 80% of a system's external use cases have been exposed and studied. Any fewer and you run the risk of not knowing enough about the system under construction. Any more and you reach diminishing returns, for you can never know everything important about a system until you start building it. As a measure of product, I measure the *number and completeness of all use cases.*[12] Even the most complex production systems seem to embody only a few dozen central scenarios, with many more variations on the theme of these central ones. If you don't find this hierarchy of primary and secondary scenarios, that you've probably have under- or overanalyzed. For instance, does your system have only one primary scenario? If so, it's either very simple, or you haven't yet understood the real problem. Do you have an 8000-page requirements document (which I've seen on a real project), but totally inadequate use-case or context analysis?

During *design*, the primary product is an architecture. This is perhaps the most critical milestone in the life of a project, for it represents putting the initial stake in the ground regarding the system's implementation. The primary measure of goodness is the validation of the first executable architectural prototype. First, consider the *coverage* of this prototype. If it touches upon most of the major architectural seams in the system, then you have built a release that has value. If it touches upon only a few seams, that you cannot necessarily trust the architecture to be a good predictor of future work, largely because you will probably be blindsided later on by implicit architectural assumptions that you made but never validated. Coverage also can be measured by the number of use cases identified during analysis that are addressed by this prototype. Second, measure the *performance* of this architecture. Even recognizing that it is vastly incomplete, a study of the system's

---

[12] Capers Jones (1994) defines the measure *number of object points,* an object point being roughly equal to one scenario in a use case.

time and space behavior now goes a long way in pointing out areas of future risk.

During *evolution*, the primary product is a stream of executable releases, each representing an evolutionary refinement of the initial architecture. In this phase, there are a number of quantifiable measures that can be made. First, measure the *number of classes* in each release; this will give you a sense of the growing size of the system. I never really use lines of code as a measure, except in the following manner. For each release, track the lines of code in the system. If you find the *line count decreasing* while the total number of classes is stable or even increasing, then this is usually a sign of a very healthy project, because it represents the fact that your developers have found a path to a simpler architecture, something they could not have *a priori* known until they were further into implementation.

SHAPE

Second, measure the shape of each release. This is where the various tactical metrics from Chidamber and Kemerer come in. To summarize, they suggest the following metrics:
- Weighted methods per class
- Depth of inheritance tree
- Number of children
- Coupling between objects
- Response for a class
- Lack of cohesion in methods

It is wrong to blindly calculate these metrics and force your team to optimize them to certain levels. Rather, they should be used collectively as a measure of health. If you find inheritance lattices that are bloated or anorexic compared with other lattices in the system, then you ought to focus some management attention on them. If you have a few classes that are statistically out-of-line with others in regards to number of methods, coupling, or cohesion, then these too need some special attention.

RISK

Third, measure certain indicators of risk in the system. Applying a simple complexity measure of all classes and identifying those that are relatively more complex than others is typically a good way to find those classes that are likely to be error-prone. Use this information to drive your formal reviews, since most projects can't afford the time or energy to walk through every class. Studying the rate at which classes change in the system is a good measure of stability, and is something that's not terribly hard to measure. Just by instrumenting your configuration management system (um, your project does have one, doesn't it?) management can get an easy measure of where there exists turmoil in the system, and thus perhaps requires the attention of a red team (or a SWAT team as some call it) to tackle this instability to the ground. In healthy projects, you will initially find instability throughout the architecture, slowly stabilizing from the core categories and then outward. Even at the latest stages of a project, some kinds of changes should be allowed and thus not viewed as threatening. For example, changing the signature of a method, or even adjusting an inheritance lattice is rarely a sign of impending doom. Ripping out entire class trees is not a good sign, however.

DEFECTS

Fourth, there are measures of defects. On of the great advantages of an evolutionary development process is that you can engage your testing team early in the life cycle, to begin to measure defect data. Because successive refinement means continuous integration, it is possible and desirable to measure defects for every release, for their trends will help point out product maturity. I generally prefer to measure defects per total classes, rather than defects per thousand lines of code, primarily because number of classes are a better predictor of system complexity. Furthermore, studies seem to suggest that there is an anticorrelation between numbers of classes and lines of code. In healthy systems, the 80/20 rule seems to apply: 80% of the software defects will be found in 20% of the system's classes. This is why measuring relative class complexity is so important.

As some parting advice, remember that gauging the health of an object-oriented system is subtly different than measuring a nonobject-oriented one, mainly because the fundamental units of decomposition differ. Clearly, it is possible to measure a multitude of properties in any system. Be careful not to generate lots of pretty numbers on charts that tell you nothing, for over time your developers will grow to resent all such numbers gathering as an intrusion upon their real work at hand. Furthermore, don't select a few key measures and blindly manage these numbers. All individual measures of goodness are just one view into the health of a system, and it requires active management to know when to ignore certain measures, and when to leap on small changes in measurements.

CHAPTER 4

PROJECTS AND TEAMS

Having a clearly-defined project, together with healthy team dynamics, are always essential ingredients to success, but object-oriented project teams present some unique challenges that Grady has addressed in various articles.

We include the following two articles in this chapter:

- *The Object-Oriented Project*[1] describes a classification of the types of OO projects and observations of these with respect to architecture, rigor of development process, documentation, and process maturity.

- *Growing Mature Abstractionists* discusses the important skill of abstraction on OO projects and the role of an abstractionist. Grady articulates what skills a good abstractionist will possess, and he describes how to recognize and cultivate abstractionists within the team.

There have also been a number of articles were incorporated into *Object Solutions*, so are not included here, but are summarized below:

- *When Bad Things Happen to Good Projects*[2] identifies certain project risks specific to OO projects and advises project teams to remain customer-focused. Grady presents a few case studies and recommendations for risk avoidance.

- *The Five Habits of Successful Object-Oriented Projects*[3] discusses how the health of project teams is often easy to spot. Grady presents the five habits and how the absence of good habits is an indicator of likely project failure. The habits are: (1) A ruthless focus on the development

---

[1] Booch, G. (1993). The object-oriented project. *Object Magazine* 3(4).

[2] Booch, G. (1994). When bad things happen to good projects. *Object Magazine* 4(2).

[3] Booch, G. (1994). The five habits of successful object-oriented projects. *Object Magazine* 4(4).

of a system that provides a well-understood collection of essential minimal characteristics. (2) The existence of a culture that is centered on results, encourages communication, and yet is not afraid to fail. (3) The effective use of object-oriented modeling. (4) The existence of a strong architectural vision. (5) The application of a well-managed iterative and incremental development life cycle.

- *Rules of Thumb*[4] helps set the team's expectations and presents project planning guidelines.

- *The Development Team*[5] discusses the critical importance of people to a project's success. There must be a reasonable distribution of responsibilities among the team, into well-defined roles, which Grady enumerates. The central role and critical responsibilities of the architect are described.

THE OBJECT-ORIENTED PROJECT

People can be divided into one of two groups: those who divide people into two groups, and those who don't.   —*Anonymous*

In trying to characterize the spread of object-oriented technology, it is possible to partition the marketplace along a number of different dimensions.[6] For example, we might differentiate among projects completed by early adopters of the technology, versus projects in the steady state carried out by organizations that have already deployed significant object-oriented systems. Along this dimension, we see significant differences in approaches to risk management. In particular, inaugural projects tend to be more open to risk, simply because a typical goal of such projects is to calibrate the risk of the technology in the context of that organization's particular culture. In contrast, steady-state projects tend to be slightly more risk averse, largely

---

[4] Booch, G. (1995). Rules of thumb. *Report on Object Analysis & Design 2*(4).

[5] Booch, G. (1995). The development team. *Report on Object Analysis & Design 1*(6).

[6] Of course, this is true of all problems of classification: The organization we chose is directly dependent upon the reasons we are doing the classification.

because some critical business venture likely depends upon the project's outcome.

Alternatively, we might divide the market according to object-oriented programming language. The cultural differences among C++, Smalltalk, and Eiffel projects, for example, are often striking. While it is unfair to apply stereotypes to any specific project, we can make some broad generalizations. For example, it is rare to find Smalltalk projects staffed with more than a couple of dozen developers; it is not uncommon to find C++ projects staffed with dozens if not a few hundred developers. Smalltalkers will thus gleefully make *ad hominem* attacks by noting the folly of large C++ projects ("Small is beautiful" is the appropriate rallying cry), but C++ers will often counter by pointing out the lack of disciplined development by some Smalltalkers. Such religious attacks are just plain silly, but for some projects they do sometimes reflect a deeper truth.

Continuing, we might divide the object-oriented marketplace by domain: management information systems versus command and control systems versus process control, and so on. Along this dimension, the presence of the object-oriented paradigm is largely felt in the form of domain-specific frameworks. This view is significant in that it offers a focus for organizations intent upon applying object-oriented technology to a particular vertical market. Thus, today, we see frameworks being developed for securities trading, patient health care, telephone switching systems, and accounting systems. Interestingly, few such domain-specific frameworks are traded on the open market: rather, they serve as a competitive advantage for the company that created them, and so have a value far greater than could be commanded on the open reuse market.

These three views are largely orthogonal: We find inaugural projects as well as more mature projects across virtually every application domain. The same is true of the scattering of languages versus application domain, although languages such as Smalltalk seem to have found a niche in securities trading, and languages such as Ada have found a niche in the transportation industry.[7]

There is yet another partitioning of the marketplace that we might consider, and it proves to be a particularly useful one because it tells us something about the maturity of the corresponding software development organization. Along this dimension, I classify each object-oriented project into one of two categories: projects that *serve the needs of isolated application development*, and projects that *encompass the activities of a whole enterprise*.

Most organizations gain early experience in the object-oriented paradigm through the development of applications that are relatively independent of the rest of the business' computing activities. This is the domain of the grass-roots developer... someone decides that object-oriented programming is a *cool thing*, and so plays with a low-cost compiler for a while, ultimately gaining enough experience to convince management to try it on some small project. Such early projects are usually characterized as only marginally disciplined, but that is not necessarily a *bad thing*, because any new technology requires some amount of exploratory development, and trying out these ideas on small projects creates an environment wherein failure is tolerated.

An aside: Don't underestimate the importance of *failure* in object-oriented development. Designing simple object-oriented architectures is hard, and I guarantee that you will have false starts in your first projects. It is better that you gain this experience early with low-risk projects, rather than betting your company on the technology the first time.

If the corresponding software development organization is sufficiently mature, early positive experience in small projects will naturally be carried over into larger ones. This is indeed a primary way that technology transfer happens in the market today. People carry with them their experience base of using object-oriented technology in the context of that organization's particular development culture.

---

[7] Many of the world's next generation air-traffic control systems are being written in Ada, and recently, the French National Railway announced a large Ada initiative. Before I get flooded with letters: Yes, I know that Ada is *not* an object-oriented programming language; according to Peter Wegner's criteria, it is object-based. Among other things, Ada95 adds features to the language so that is may truly be called object oriented.

My rather unscientific data gathering suggests that most organizations are just at this cusp of changeover with regard to object-oriented technology. With a growing body of experience as to the real (as opposed to imagined) benefits of objects, we see more companies, rather than individual development projects, beginning to embrace the technology at an enterprise-wide level.

However, some organizations never grow beyond this independent/isolated project stage, and are content to apply object-oriented technology to new projects of growing complexity, without consideration for the leverage that objects might provide across projects. This leads me to suggest the primary litmus test for classifying projects along their object-oriented maturity: isolated application development tends to focus on building relatively independent applications very well; whereas enterprise-wide development tends to focus on building families of programs.

There are a number of important implications that derive from this distinction with respect to a team's interest in architecture, process, and documentation.

- Perhaps foremost is the degree of focus upon *architecture*. Isolated application development tends to have only secondary concern for architecture, and unfortunately, tools that support that domain only encourage this view of the world. Development environments such as Microsoft's Visual C++, for example, provide wizards that eliminate some of the tedium of object-oriented development, but they also force you down to the details of a particular framework very quickly, making it difficult to raise your head above water to see a larger architectural vision of the program you are trying to build.[8] More mature organizations respect the importance of architecture, and in some manner institutionalize it, typically by identifying and empowering a chief architect. Indeed, among those organizations I have seen that have tried to apply enterprise-wide object-oriented computing, those that neglect a

---

[8] This is not meant as an attack on Microsoft's development products, or any similar tool; I'm not a tools bigot, and will use whatever tool makes sense to get my job done. Especially on the PC, however, many such development environments do not encourage an architectural view of the system under development.

system's architecture tend to fail. Why is this so? Simply stated, the central problem in building families of programs is not so much in crafting beautifully designed classes, but is more so a problem of crafting patterns of collaborative classes. These patterns do not just happen; they must be consciously architected and carried out consistently.

- Another implication concerns the *rigor of the development process*. In isolated application development, the process is dominated by the personalities of the individual developers. This is not to say that this is a horrible practice: some of the world's most innovative software has sprung from the collective minds of a small, informal merry band of developers. However, this practice does not scale to enterprise-wide computing, nor does it work to achieve a predictable, sustainable software development effort. Those organizations that try to make this transition to enterprise-wide object-oriented computing without considering a more formal process tend to fail. At the other extreme, those organizations that try to leap to enterprise-wide processes without validating their process on smaller real projects also tend to fail. Of course, every organization has to find a balance between too much rigor and not enough. This has important implications for management: enterprise-wide object-oriented computing requires active management involvement, because the kinds of products and measures of goodness tend to be subtly different for object-oriented systems than for traditional processes. In the steady state, we can characterize the process of mature organizations as one of generating a steady stream of successive refinements to an architecture. This task is made particularly challenging in the face of a family of programs, because one must make risk trade-offs that may be suboptimal for certain individual programs, although optimal for the business at large. For example, the decision to use a particular object [database] management system might subvert the previous decisions of one ongoing project, although in the long run, across the enterprise, it might lead to considerable savings because of the use of common patterns.

- Continuing, organizations that seek to build families of programs tend to view *documentation* very differently than their counterparts building isolated applications. For enterprise-wide computing, documentation must encompass the rationale of the architecture, if we are to ever build enduring systems that transcend the lifetimes of their creators. Documentation standards thus tend to be much more formal, and in fact, documentation is often treated as an important, reviewable deliverable. Isolated applications, on the other hand, do not represent such a capital investment in software, and so it is often more economical to throw people at the problem rather than properly document the system's design. Of course, the very real tendency is for larger projects to be documentation obsessed, thus (incorrectly) focusing upon documentation products at the expense of software products. Similarly, isolated application development tends to be product-driven, at the expense of writing meaningful documentation. In any case, a balance is required: the successful projects in both categories tend to view documentation as an important derived product of the development process. How many of you have programming style guides? Most would answer *yes*. How many of you have architectural style guides? Unfortunately, most would answer *no*, although such documents are essential in crafting families of programs.

Does this mean that enterprise-wide object-oriented computing is the desired end point for every mature development organization? Not necessarily. To remain nimble in the marketplace, you have to know when to establish corporate guidelines and when to break them. However, the level of maturity that successful enterprise-wide computing represents is something to strive for. Object-oriented stuff is indeed a *cool thing*, but ultimately most of us are in the business to make real projects with whatever resources we can find. We tend to get the most leverage from object-orientation when we apply these concepts to building frameworks, and this can only happen if we raise our heads from our workstations from time to time, and recognize the need for a mature development process.

GROWING MATURE ABSTRACTIONISTS

Try the following exercise with the members of your budding object-oriented development organization: Generate a class hierarchy, given the following objects drawn from the domain of an information model for an insurance company—an insurance policy, a whole life policy, a universal life policy, a personal liability policy, an automobile insurance policy, and a property insurance policy.

(Now we all wait while the theme song from "Jeopardy" plays.)

You will get a variety of responses.... Some of your developers, especially those who have not yet engaged in the world of object-oriented stuff, may respond with the question, "So, what's a class?" Your truly object-oriented developers might produce a tidy class hierarchy, illustrating the generalization/specialization of various classes of these objects. Your more seasoned developers will likely go further by introducing some intermediate abstract classes, (such as the class "life insurance,") whose presence serves to simplify the hierarchy by providing a locus for certain common structure or common behavior. Your wild-eyed object-oriented zealots—look around, every company seems to have one of two of these types lurking about—will immediately launch into an impassioned plea as to why multiple inheritance is absolutely essential for such a problem, and will then sit down and hack out an executable prototype that defends their point of view.

Well, all of the above responses are wrong.

The "right" reply to this exercise is not a tidy class hierarchy, nor an elegant one, nor a running prototype, but rather, another question: "Why am I building this hierarchy?" Meaningful abstractions can never be crafted in the absence of a well-defined context. Stated more intensely, any such abstraction that we try to build without knowing why we are making this classification is usually vacuous, over-engineered, or both.

Given the following three objects, which is the most different: a trout, a cow, or a lungfish? If I'm developing an information model for a restaurant,

I'd probably say that the lungfish is the most different, since it's the one object of the three you'd likely never see on a menu. If I'm developing an information model for an aquarium, I'd probably choose the cow. (Gary Larson, cartoonist for the Far Side, might disagree with me, but I've never seen a cow particularly skilled in doing the breast stroke, or the butterfly. Besides, who would pay money to see trained cows perform at Sea World?) If I'm studying the underlying genetic structure of these three objects, I'd likely select the trout as most different, since as it turns out, the cow and lung fish appear to be relatively close in their evolutionary development.

Ask different biologists how many species there are, and you will get answers that range from 2 million to 50 million. It all depends upon why you are producing a particular classification.

Classification is *the central problem* in all things object oriented. Classification is indeed at the root of the problem of identifying classes and objects, the first step in many approaches to object-oriented analysis and design. However, classification is hard. There is no magic available to automatically craft a profound class or class hierarchy: These tasks require individual creativity, intuition, and experience. Unfortunately, not everyone is good at it.

My term for an analyst or developer gifted with skills in classification is an *abstractionist*. I have an unscientific rule of thumb that says, given a group of developers, only about 20-30% of them are probably really good at object-oriented abstraction. That doesn't mean that the remaining 70-80% are bad, evil, or inadequate programmers. Rather, it is a recognition of the fact that some people are better than others at looking at the world and discovering or inventing abstractions of reality.

This is actually good news. Not everyone on a development team should be an abstractionist. I have seen more than a few object-oriented projects fail because every developer was almost equally skilled in classification, and as such, the team could never get consensus about the right collection of classes for the problem at hand. The principal symptom of such projects is that their architecture never stabilizes, because there are constant debates about whether or not certain seams in the system are expressed at the proper level of abstraction.

Another reason this is good news is that it's a recognition of the different skill sets that many organizations have in place. Many smaller development shops are more homogeneous, but larger organizations tend to have a wide mixture of skills, ranging from earthy assembly language programmers, to elitist programmers working in avant-garde languages, to analysts, and to architects.

Not everyone on a team needs to be an abstractionist, although some must be skilled at classification. Fortunately, these skills appear to be something that can be learned, although some are born abstractionists, just as some seem born to be artists.

My observation is that a good abstractionist embodies at least the following three skills:

- First, he or she usually has a *good intuition for the clean separation of concerns* between any two given abstractions. The classical object-oriented example of an object under a GUI system knowing how to draw itself is simplistic, in that it implies a close coupling between the object being displayed and the agent that offers a protocol for how the object displays itself. The abstractionist recognizes that a coupling indeed exists, and strives to separate the responsibilities of these two entities so that the assumptions each makes about the other are well-defined. This so-called contract model of programming, as suggested by Bertrand Meyer, is something that the skilled abstractionist practices regularly.

- Second, the abstractionist is also *a behaviorist*, meaning that he or she can look beyond the structural attributes of an entity, and see its behavior in the world. A life insurance policy is more than just a record of the policy holder, the beneficiary, and the terms of the policy; each of these objects play a role in the context of some problem, and exhibits a behavior that distinguishes it from all other structurally similar abstractions. A life insurance policy may be redeemed, it may be canceled, its beneficiaries may be changed. These are all behaviors that define the abstraction, and hence are something that the skilled abstractionist should be able to draw out from the context of the problem.

- Third, a good abstractionist is *articulate*. Abstractionists who serve as analysts, meaning that they are responsible for setting the desired behavior of the system, must work with end users and domain experts who likely do not understand the possibilities and limitations of an automated solution and who likely don't even themselves understand what they want their system to do. To blame the failure of a system on the excuse that its users never expressed clear requirements is usually an infantile response. One clear responsibility of the abstractionist as an analyst is to draw these requirements out and establish where the areas of uncertainty exist. This requires that the abstractionist be able to communicate well. Similarly, abstractionists who serve as designers must be able to take this object-oriented view of the problem domain, and translate it into something that other developers, who may have little domain knowledge, can understand. This too requires good communication skills. The developers I encounter who produce the most arcane code are often those who can't even write a decent e-mail message.[9]

I should note that the most mature abstractionists are those who seem to be able to recognize patterns that transcend individual classes.

How can an organization identify the abstractionists who exist in their midst? I often use a very simple technique: CRC cards. The use of CRC cards has a number of documented benefits (some call CRC cards the poor man's object-oriented CASE tool), but one importance consequence of using them is that they serve to segment your developers. Specifically, you'll find some of your team really get engaged in a CRC card session, while others

---

[9] (Of course, there are always exceptions to this rule of thumb. I've met a handful of really world-class programmers who are, for the most part, the silent type, but their productivity is ten- to a hundredfold that of most mortals. I am always in awe of such folks. My theory is that these people are such intense thinkers, that there is an impedance mismatch between the speed of their mind and the pace of the rest of the world. If your organization is graced to have one or more of these stellar individuals, hang on to them dearly. Or, if you can't hang on to them, send me their resume...)

will sit on the sidelines. While this is not always a litmus test for abstraction-ists (someone might be unengaged because his/her goldfish just died, or was up too late the night before, either partying or programming), those who do engage are often the ones who are excited about and good at discovering abstractions of the real world.

How can an organization grow an abstractionist? Well, as I said earlier, the important lesson is that abstraction can indeed be learned, and this flows from what I call the Nike school of software development: *just do it.* In other words, an abstractionist grows by developing more abstractions. This approach has two important implications. If you need to jump start your organization, perhaps because it is just beginning to leap into the object-ori-ented waters, you need to introduce a mentoring programming. This means introducing some more experienced object-oriented developers (from out-side the company, or from internal groups who have completed an object-oriented pilot project) who serve to guide the work of the budding abstrac-tionist. At first, this means exposing the neophyte developer to good object-oriented code and designs. As time unfolds, this means guiding the devel-opers in using good abstractions, then eventually writing new ones of their own. The beauty of this approach is that it is self-sustaining: once you have a few good abstractionists, they can in turn mentor other promising neophyte abstractionists.

The second implication of this approach is that the development organi-zation must understand the role of *failure.* The Mona Lisa was not the first work of da Vinci; he had drawn thousands of images earlier in his career. So it is with classification: profound classifications are rare, clumsy ones are common, and so we must strive for writing at least some good ones. This comes about only if the developer has the opportunity and the time to try alternatives, and rejects those that just don't work. Now, this is a scary pros-pect: Most projects don't think they have time to throw things away. Rather, such projects tend to view code as a very precious commodity, something that *the (electronic) pen having writ, the pen moves on....* Of course, this is not reality. If an abstraction is genuinely bad and allowed to persist unchanged, it will fester and eventually become a cancer that disfigures the entire architecture. For this reason, we must take a pragmatic view of failure:

Sometimes is it the right business decision to stick with a less-than-good abstraction, but only if one understands the risks and consequences therein. A good abstractionist can make such a trade-off, and one grows such abstractionists by letting them suffer the consequences of their own abstractions.

CHAPTER 5

MODELS

One of the challenges for any methodologist is to balance the needs for expressiveness and clarity, while adopting what techniques that are successful in industry practice. Booch has sought this balance, adopting many of the best practices in the industry. Because it is both pragmatic and expressive, the Booch Method has achieved widespread international use. Collectively, the Booch Method, OMT, and with OOSE/Objectory, are the most used methods worldwide. The Booch Method has been successfully applied in many industries and at many levels of abstraction. The biggest Booch fans are those who require its rich notation; it has been especially popular in software engineering-intensive projects. Such projects are often global in scope, require distributed and concurrent processing, and operate in heterogeneous environments.

In this chapter, we present several of Grady's articles dealing with notation and semantics, including their history, evolution, and future.

- The first article, *Why We Model,*[1] addresses why models are essential, especially for understanding and building systems of any complexity. Grady discusses lessons on how to model, including the need to model a given design with multiple, nearly independent, perspectives.

- *The Evolution of the Booch Method*[2] appeared in the premier issue of ROAD in 1994, before Jim Rumbaugh and Ivar Jacobson joined Rational. Grady discusses how the Booch Method evolved, adopting the industry's best practices.

---

[1] Based on Booch, G. (1996). Why we model. *Object Magazine, 9*(9).

[2] Based on Booch, G. (1994). The evolution of the Booch Method. *Report on Object Analysis & Design, 1*(1).

- *Next Generation Methods*[3] discusses similarities between existing OO methods, and presents common elements that all OO methods must provide.

- *Unification*[4] describes the history of OOA&D methods, and how "natural selection" played a large role in its evolution. Grady describes how Jim Rumbaugh and Ivar Jacobson's joining Rational greatly accelerated the process of industry unification.

- *Quality Software and the Unified Modeling Language*[5] discusses how the process behind developing UML has being driven by quality concerns. Grady discusses the need for a balance between clarity and the need to explicitly model architecture, which are critical to project success.

A few additional comments on the UML are in order here. As of the writing of this book in the late summer of 1996, the UML was in a draft 0.9 state. Via more than a thousand e-mail messages to OTUG[6] or directly to Jim, Ivar, and Grady, the industry provided their feedback on the 0.8 and 0.9 drafts. The "Three Amigos" (as they call themselves) also have had intensive conversations with other industry methodologists and companies applying various methods. Rational plans to respond to the Object Management Group's[7] request-for-proposal asking for a standard OO metamodel and notation with the UML by the end of January, 1997. Microsoft, HP, and others will join in this submission to the OMG. Although there are competing perspectives, none of them have the international following of the UML. Even so, these other perspectives will undoubtedly

---

[3] Based on Booch, G. (1993). "Next Generation Methods," which appeared in the *Object-Oriented Analysis & Design: Finding Your Path* supplement to *Object Magazine* and other SIGS Publications in late 1993.

[4] Based on Booch, G. (1996). Unification. *Object Magazine, 6*(2).

[5] Based on an article that was originally published on the World Wide Web in early 1996.

[6] OTUG is the Object Technology Users Group established at OOPSLA 1995 for discussion on methods. To enroll in its e-mail forum, send an e-mail to *majordomo@rational.com* with the following line in the body: *subscribe otug.*

[7] OMG is a standards-adopting organization, most known for the CORBA standard. See *http://www.omg.org.*

strengthen the industry's decisions. The OMG is scheduled to endorse a standard OO metamodel and notation (optionally) by July 1997. The latest and most complete information on the UML can be obtained from Rational Software's web site, *http://www.rational.com.*

In addition to articles on the general evolution of methods, Booch has, of course, written on specific notation topics. The following are included in this chapter:

- *Scenarios*[8] describes the critical role of scenarios as a driver of the development process, and the notations supporting them.

- *Properties and Stereotypes*[9] presents two additional concepts that Booch et al. recently adopted for inclusion into the UML.

- *Finite State Machines*[10] covers the FSM notation used in the UML.

In addition to these, we present several notation and semantic topics in the next chapter on Architecture as well, including distributed systems, patterns, protocols, and interfaces.

WHY WE MODEL

Well over a decade ago, Edward Tufte published his seminal book, *The Visual Display of Quantitative Information* (Tufte 1983), on the topic of data graphics. As he defines it, the purpose of data graphics is to "visually display measured quantities by means of the combined use of points, lines, a coordinate system, numbers, symbols, words, shading, and color (p. 9)." He goes on to note that "graphics reveal data (p. 13)." In other words, faced with a complex set of information, well-chosen symbols can make that information

---

[8] Based on Booch, G. (1994). Scenarios. *Report on Object Analysis & Design, 1*(3).
[9] Based on Booch, G. (1996). Properties and Stereotypes. *Report on Object Analysis & Design, 2*(5).
[10] Based on Booch, G. (1995). Real-time systems. *Report on Object Analysis & Design, 1*(5).

accessible and understandable, and even offer insights that simply cannot be made when staring at the raw data itself.

So it is with software. There are patterns of design that cannot be discerned just by staring at lines of code. For example, I might encounter the following statement in Java:

```
s.Handle(m);
```

Not very revealing. However, if I know that this code is part of an occurrence of the chain of responsibility pattern,[11] then suddenly I know volumes: this particular line deals with the delegation of a message to a successor object. Patterns such as this reveal themselves only when viewed at higher levels of abstraction. In fact, all well-structured object-oriented software is full of patterns, and this elegance of structure can only be seen when we study our raw code using the language of patterns.

Tufte later observes that "what is to be sought in designs for the display of information is the clear portrayal of complexity; not the complication of the simple; rather the task of the designer is to give visual access to the subtle and the difficult—that is, the revelation of the complex (Tufte 1993, 191)." Although Tufte was not talking about software, his remarks are certainly applicable here. Software is one of the most complex of human artifacts, and especially in a system of scale, there is so much inherent complexity that the only way to even begin to understand it is to view it from a number of different and nearly independent perspectives. This then the essence of why we model:

> *We build models of complex systems because we*
> *cannot comprehend any such system in its*
> *entirety.*

There are limits to the human ability to understand complexity. Through modeling, we achieve two things. First, we narrow the problem we are

---

[11] Chain of responsibility is one of the patterns found in the Gang of Four's book, *Design Patterns*.

studying by focusing on only one aspect at a time. This is essentially the approach of divide-and-conquer that Dijkstra spoke of years ago: attack a hard problem by dividing it into a series of smaller problems that you can solve. Second, by modeling we can amplify the human intellect. A model properly chosen can let the modeler work at higher levels of abstraction: this is what Hofstadter calls chunking.

Saying one ought to model does not necessarily make it happen. In fact, a number of surveys suggest that most software development teams do little or no formal modeling. Plot the use of modeling against the complexity of a project, and you'll find that the simpler the project, the less likely it is that modeling will be used. However, as I've written many times, software systems are in general getting more and more complex, and this is causing more and more organizations to start modeling in order to give a "clear portrayal of complexity."

Recently, I returned from addressing a large conference for users of a certain very popular 4GL. A number of developers there told me of hitting the wall: their tools worked well with little or no modeling, but only if they were below a certain threshold of complexity. Further, there were forces in their domain that were bringing them closer and closer to that threshold with each new project. Once they crossed that threshold, if they had done no modeling, the meltdown scenario was always the same: the resulting system was so brittle and so hard to understand that each new feature or requirement change was always exponentially harder to implement than the last. At some point, diminishing returns would be reached, meaning that it became easier to toss the entire system and start over rather than to continue to evolve it.

Let me be clear: not every project requires modeling. However, the more complex your project is, the more likely you will fail or the more likely you will build the wrong thing if you do no modeling. Further, all interesting systems have a natural tendency to become more complex. Thus, although you might think you don't need to model today, as your system evolves, you will learn to regret that decision, long after it is too late.

Having lived through a number of large projects, some of which did a good job of modeling and some of which did no modeling whatsoever, let me offer four lessons on how to model.

The choice of what models to create has a profound influence upon how a problem is attacked and how a solution is shaped.

Ignoring software for a moment, suppose I'm trying to tackle a problem in quantum physics. Certain problems, like the interaction of photons in space-time, are full of wonderfully hairy mathematics. Chose a different model than the raw calculus, and all of a sudden this inherent complexity melts away. This is precisely the value of Feynman diagrams, which provide a graphical rendering of a very complex problem. Similarly, suppose I'm constructing a new building, and I'm concerned about how it might behave in high winds. If I build a physical model and then subject it to wind tunnel tests, I might learn some interesting things. On the other hand, if I build a mathematical model and then subject it to simulations, I might learn some other things (and also probably be able to play with more new scenarios than if I were using physical models). Models being what they are, I'd be safest if I built both the physical model and the mathematical model, since they each would have been built and studied with different sets of assumptions.

In software, what models we chose to make greatly affects our world view. If I build a system through the eyes of a database developer, I'll end up with an entity-oriented schema that pushes behavior into triggers and stored procedures. If I build a system through the eyes of a structured analyst, then I'll end up with a system that's algorithmic-centric, with data flowing from process to process. If I build a system through the eyes of an object-oriented developer, then I'll end up with a system whose architecture is centered around a sea of classes and the patterns of interaction that animate those classes. Any one of these might be right for a given application and a given development culture. However, the point is that each world view leads to a very different kind of system with different costs and benefits.

Continuing,

> *No single model is sufficient; every complex*
> *system is best approached through a small set of*
> *nearly independent models.*

If I'm constructing a building, there is no single set of blueprints that reveals its subtleties. At the very least, I'll probably need floor plans, elevations, electrical plans, plumbing plans, and so on.

The operative phrase here is *nearly independent.* This is a term that come from Herbert Simon, and in this context means having models that can be built and studied separately, but that are interrelated. As in the building, one can study electrical plans in isolation, but these have a mapping to the floor plans, and probably interact with the plumbing plans.

In object-oriented software systems, our experience suggests that there are 4 + 1 views that are relevant. We say "4 + 1" rather than just "5" to emphasize the idea that there are four primary views and one overarching view that serves to integrate them. The four primary views include:

- *Logical view* — The classes of a system, together with their patterns of collaboration

- *Concurrency view* — The processes and threads that animate the classes of the logical view

- *Implementation view* — The concrete manifestation of the logical and tasking elements

- *Deployment view* — The platform upon which these elements exist

and the "+ 1" view is:

- *Scenario view* — The use cases that specify the behavior of the system

The interesting thing about these different views is that they force the development team to concentrate upon the strategic as well as the tactical decisions that are relevant to object-oriented systems.

Experience with object-oriented modeling also suggests the following:

*Every model may be expressed at different levels
of fidelity.*

Sometimes you need a 35,000 foot view of a system, and sometimes you have to get down and dirty with the bits. The best kinds of models are those that let you do either, depending upon why you need to view it and upon who doing the viewing. An analyst or an end user will want to focus on issues of *what,* whereas an implementer will need to focus on issues of *how,* and even both of these stakeholders will want to visualize a system at different levels of detail.

This connectedness suggests one final lesson about how to model:

The best models are connected to reality.

The Achilles heel of structured analysis techniques is the fact that there is a basic disconnect between analysis views and design views. Failing to bridge this chasm would mean that the system as conceived and the system as built would diverge over time. In object-oriented modeling, it is possible to connect all the nearly-independent views of a system into one semantic whole.

THE EVOLUTION OF THE BOOCH METHOD

Call me a software therapist if you like, but I find it fascinating to step into a project and assess its reaction to object-oriented analysis and design methods. At one end of the spectrum, I find software anarchists who proudly share their detest of any and all methods, claiming that they stifle creativity. In some of these projects, even object-oriented languages such as C++ and Smalltalk are viewed with disdain because—so they claim—they offer nothing that can't already be done in a lower-level language such as C. This model of software development gives rise to the image of the rugged software cowboy who rides into town armed only with a high-performance PC and single-handedly creates a killer app that redefines the entire industry. For a number of complex reasons, this attitude seems most prevalent in the United States, although, believe me, it is by no means unique to this country. (My own highly unscientific survey shows that this mentality is most often found in small and large companies in cities, towns, and rural areas located near large bodies of water, mountains, or plains. I don't know, I think that there's a pattern in there somewhere...) For many, the lone software cowboy cuts an appealing, almost heroic figure, sustained by a few apocryphal rags-to-riches stories of various software entrepreneurs.

In all honesty, this anarchist's model does work from time to time and thus, pragmatically speaking, is an approach worthy of consideration when intense innovation is required. However, software anarchy is by no means a sustainable business process. Because the resulting software products are rarely scaleable, extensible, portable, or reusable, the long-term cost of ownership of such products is intolerably high. There is also a high social cost. From time to time, it's genuinely fun to be part of a tightly focused, high-energy, independent band of software outlaws, but it's rarely a life-style that can be endured forever.

At the other end of the spectrum, I find projects that turn methods into a minor religion. There is often much hand wringing and ceremony attached to the selection of *The Method* for the company. Factions in the organization arise, each clinging to one particular method and defending its position with emotional zeal. In the worst of all possible cases, the company's middle management is so insecure about its ability to cope with this new object-oriented stuff, that the selected method gets wrapped in layers of management such that the development process as well as the content of all nonsoftware products (especially all analysis and design documentation and development reports) are laid out in excruciating detail. The usual diagnosis is a case of bureaucracy gone mad in the face of objects.

Typically, the project management team in these kinds of projects really does have all the right intentions, with its work carried out all in the name of providing a mature development process. However, by overcontrolling the development organization, management ultimately ends up stifling all creativity. In effect, this model of development encourages exactly that which it intends to counter, namely, the establishment of the software cowboy mentality. In order for its developers to get any real work done, they must flaunt the management-imposed method and do their work in the underground, again at the expense of a sustainable business process.

Most organizations fall somewhere in between these two end points of the spectrum. The healthy projects I encounter have found a place for the software cowboy, usually corralling them to work on future product issues, or high-risk, ongoing projects that need a jolt of raw technical innovation. Healthy projects also take a calm attitude toward control: recognizing that the most important product of a software development organization is software, all other non-software products are viewed as artifacts that serve either as a lasting legacy of the architecture or as a management tool that can be used to direct the development process itself.

Let me be very pragmatic: To build a sustainable business, an organization *must* chose some development method, and adapt it to its own particular culture. If your company doesn't have an identifiable development process, the absolute best thing you can do is just chose one. If you do have an identifiable development process, the absolute best thing you can do is keep improving it by incorporating new elements from emerging work, and throwing away those parts that don't actively contribute the organization's primary mission, namely, delivering good software.

This is where methodologists such as myself play a role. Having been involved in a multitude of object-oriented projects all over the globe, from telephone systems to management decision systems to embedded controllers, you quickly begin to discover what works and what doesn't. To a large extent, the purpose of a method is to codify these good practices, and to provide a common language of expression so that developers can communicate within and among teams. With the Booch Method in particular, I've sought to provide a notation and process that is especially suited to the development of object-oriented software.

The Booch Method today can fairly be called a second-generation object-oriented analysis and design method. It provides a unification of my earlier work with elements from Objectory, OMT, and other methods. The Booch Method strongly emphasizes an incremental and iterative development process. For analysis, scenarios (adopted from Objectory's concepts of use cases) are applied to capture and specify a system's desired behavior. For design, the method emphasizes the importance of architecture in terms of class structure (represented by class diagrams) and collaborations of objects (represented by object diagrams and interaction diagrams). The set of semantics of the Booch Method is effectively a superset of Objectory and OMT, and in fact borrows many specific notational elements from these and other methods. The process of the Booch Method has been formalized to support higher levels of the SEI model of software process maturity, and to address the needs of standards such as ISO 9000 for certifiable software.

Let me explain how my work has evolved by building upon experience and the contributions of my fellow methodologists, and how it likely will continue to evolve in the future.

The story of the Booch Method begins around 1982, at which time I published perhaps the first article on object-oriented development. At that time, most of my work was spent helping to architect several complex distributed systems that typically involved modest-sized databases, some real-time elements, and requirements that forced system integration with significant amounts of legacy code. Structured methods simply didn't have the expressiveness necessary to deal with this complexity, and so I sought to find a better way. By the early '80s, the theory of abstract data types had matured sufficiently to warrant its application to mission-critical systems. Smalltalk had already been on the scene for a short while, and the AI community in particular was flirting with a plethora of object-oriented variants of Lisp, many of which were inspired by the ideas in Simula. C++ hadn't been born yet, although Stroustrup was working on its conception through its predecessor, C with Classes (which evolved to be called C++ around 1983/84).

I found myself being drawn into different application areas, such as technical problems involving massive amounts of FORTRAN, management information systems involving even more massive amounts of COBOL, and applications that required a significant amount of sophisticated GUI features—and this was before the time that GUI builders had become commonplace. In retrospect, what was happening was that folks in these domains were simply running into development walls as the complexity of their systems grew larger and larger, and some were finding that my generic object-oriented design ideas had a place in solving their problems. In other words, the OO paradigm scaled better to larger systems.

For most of the rest of the 1980s, I spent my time refining these ideas and working with numerous projects, mainly in the United States and Europe, to apply them to real problems. In the second half of the '80s, virtually all of my work had migrated to C++ and Smalltalk, as those languages began to mature and tools became available. Starting in 1988, I set out to codify the notation and process of my method, which culminated in the 1990 publication of *Object-Oriented Design with Applications.*[12]

The success of this work surprised me, and I found more projects around the globe trying to apply its ideas than I could keep count of. However, frankly, I was not satisfied. There was more work to be done in defining a mature object-oriented development process that dealt with the practical issues of metrics, testing, and risk management. The method needed to be extended to deal with the problems of requirements definition and analysis. There were unresolved issues in the object-oriented programming language community that required the notation to be overly general.

Since the publication of this first-edition work, there have been three major agents of change that have caused the further maturation of the Booch Method, namely, experiences from projects using the Method, apparent consolidation in the object-oriented programming language community, and ideas from others methodologists.

The influence of experience should be obvious: Projects using the Method were usually very open about telling me what worked for them and what didn't, and I in turn actively encouraged users of the Method to communicate with me so that I could improve the Method over time. The most often cited

---

[12] This book was published in the calendar year of 1990, but due to funky publishing practices, its copyright date was 1991. For this reason, I refer to this work as Booch'91.

strengths of the Method included its focus on architecture and a sufficiently expressive notation that had a clear coupling to implementation issues. The most often cited weaknesses of the Method included the complexity of the notation and its apparent lack of a recommended life-cycle process, especially for analysis.

At the time of Booch'91, it was not clear which object-oriented programming language was going to "win" the language wars. In the late '80s there was literally an explosion of new object-oriented programming languages, but only a few were likely to survive and enter the mainstream of mission-critical development. In Booch'91, I hedged my bets by showing examples in Ada, Object Pascal, C++, Smalltalk, and CLOS. By the early '90s it became evident that C++ would emerge as the dominant language, for a variety of technical, social, political, and emotional reasons that are beyond the scope this article. (This does not mean that I think that all other languages are losers. Ada, Eiffel, Objective C, CLOS, and others have a worthy place to play in building real systems.) There was during that period a very real belief that Smalltalk would disappear from the scene altogether, although now it is apparent that Smalltalk has carved a significant place in object-oriented computing, most often being found in the client side of client/sever applications. Given this shakedown of the languages marketplace, it was possible to tune the method to map more tightly to these implementation languages.

Very close to the publication of Booch'91, the first crop of other object-oriented analysis and design method books began to pop up. Shlaer and Mellor's work predated Booch'91 slightly, OMT appeared shortly after Booch'91, Objectory emerged about a year later. What was fascinating to me is how much more alike these methods were than they were different. (Rumbaugh et al. make a similar comment in *Object-Oriented Modeling and Design*, in which they points out that my method and OMT are more alike than they are different.) Still, each new contribution brought a useful set of ideas to the community, and there was much to be learned from each one. By my count in 1993, I found about 40 or so distinct identifiable object-oriented methods, although a small number (Booch, OMT, Objectory, Shlaer/Mellor) seemed to have the most number of users worldwide. This situation was not very much different from the early days of structured analysis and design methods, at which time there were several competing alternatives.

Given these pressures, it was evident to me that a second-generation method was both possible and highly desirable. It was *possible* in the sense that there had been sufficient experience with the Method and with languages such as C++ and Smalltalk on real projects to warrant the incorporation of ideas that would simplify yet expand the applicability of the Method. It was *highly desirable* in the sense that the computing community was in a state of disarray over which object-oriented method was "best" given the plethora of methods that were similar yet different. Consolidation of methods at this time would help to expand the object-oriented industry by providing a common notation and process that could eliminate the gratuitous differences among various methods, simplify the work of tool builders, and provide some stability for more conservative development organizations moving into object-oriented technology for the first time.

Starting in 1992, I set out to specify this second-generation method, making certain to validate the ideas in real projects first before foisting them upon the world. This culminated in the publication in calendar year 1993 (copyright year 1994) of the second edition, now titled *Object-Oriented Analysis and Design with Applications*. The word *Analysis* was added to make a clear statement that the method was applicable to the front end of the lifecycle as well.

Figure 1 illustrates the contributions to this second-generation work. My explicit goals were twofold: to provide a unified notation and semantics which incorporated the best ideas from my earlier work and other widely-used methods, and to address the process and pragmatics of the Method in far greater detail.

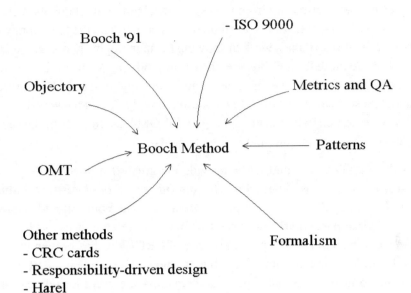

Figure 1. Influences on the Booch Method.

The Booch Method draws most heavily upon Booch'91, but where possible, simplifies the notation (certain icons, most notably for relationships, were given simpler representations; also, in the spirit of unification, rectangles were authorized as alternatives to clouds[13]).

Moving counterclockwise in the Figure, note that the most important methodological influences upon Booch'94 come from *Objectory* and *OMT*. From Objectory, I have outright adopted the ideas of use cases and Jacobson's notation for interaction diagrams. My adoption acknowledges the fact that use-case ideas work extremely well for discovering and then specifying the behavior of a system during analysis. From OMT, I have

---

[13] If there is one emotional issue in these method wars, it certainly has to do with the shape of basic class icons: Booch uses clouds, OMT uses rectangles, Objectory uses circles, Coad/Yourdon uses rounded rectangles. I chose to use clouds to represent something fundamentally different than the usual rectangles and circles, because those good symbols were already so heavily overloaded with meaning from the structured community. If you like clouds, by all means use clouds. If you like rectangles, then draw rectangles in place of clouds; I personally prefer clouds, because even in OMT, rectangles have an overloaded meaning. Except for icon shape, the Booch notation is a virtual superset of elements in the object model for methods such as OMT.

adopted elements primarily from its object model notation (elements such as associations, keys, constraints, attributed associations, and the like), many of which derive from Blaha's work in showing the mapping from object models into database models, and thus are critical in modeling systems that have a large database element. Again, rather than invent anything new, I've chosen to adopt these elements of the OMT notation directly. Along the way, I found a few ways to generalize even some parts of OMT (such as applying constraints to a variety of other modeling elements).

Although Objectory and OMT provide the greatest influences upon my latest work, I have also learned much from *other methodologists*, including Wirfs-Brock, Embley, Odell, Lorenz, Berard, Coad/Yourdon and Shlaer/ Mellor. Three particularly important influences are shown in the Figure. From Cunningham and Beck, the practice of CRC cards has proven to be a useful idea in brainstorming about objects, and so I've made it a part of the Method. From Wirfs-Brock, Rubin, and Adams—a group I loosely call the behaviorists—came the ideas of the importance of roles and responsibilities during development. From Harel—who is not exactly an object-oriented methodologist—came the ideas and notation for hierarchical state machines. Harel's work was also part of OMT, but OMT only included a subset of the full notation. I chose to return to first principles and include the larger body of Harel's work, including elements such as history and selection, which are particularly important in dealing with many kinds of reactive systems.

The importance of *formalisms* has played a small, yet significant role in the evolution of the Method. To encourage tool builders and eliminate confusion over the semantics of the notation (a problem that still plagues the structured analysis community today), I set out to precisely specify the syntax and semantics of the Booch notation. Independently, a colleague has shown a mapping of important elements of the notation into the formal language Object-Z. This explicit formalism hopefully will offer a basis for future work in transformation systems and issues of correctness.

Continuing, the so-called *patterns* movement in the object-oriented community has been an influence upon the Method as well. All well-structured object-oriented systems are full of patterns, which represent common collaborations of objects. Indeed, patterns are a central part of crafting reusable frameworks and object-oriented architectures in general. The Booch Method encourages this view of system development by providing notational elements for illustrating these kinds of collaborations, and in addition, introduces pattern creation and scavenging as an important part of the process. The Method also adopts a useful piece of notation from the work of Gamma et al., namely, a note icon that may be use to adorn any other item with arbitrary details, such as SQL statements, reports, and the like.

With the general maturation of the object-oriented community, independent work in object-oriented *metrics* and *quality assurance* has begun to emerge. Since such measures are critical to the creation of a well-managed and mature process, I sought out to incorporate those metrics that added value to the process and were proven as useful on real projects. Thus, the Method adopts work from the MIT Sloan School of Management by Chidamber and Kemerer. More recently, McCabe has proposed a set of useful object-oriented metrics that are similar in spirit to the MIT work.

Finally, experience with the SEI *process maturity* models led me to explicitly state the process of the Booch Method in a form that was defensibly high up the food chain in the SEI model. Requirements of emerging standards such as *ISO 9000* were a forcing function as well. As a result of these two influences, the second-generation Method now specifies the process of object-oriented development in detail, providing a statement of the goals, products, activities, and measures of goodness for each step of development.

One might worry that the resulting Booch notation is too complex. It is not: I can teach any software developer, manager, or end user in about half an hour a proper subset of the notation—what I call *Booch lite*—which encompasses perhaps 70-80% of the object modeling problems you will encounter. Every other advanced element in the notation is treated as an adornment, to be learned only as the semantics of your model demands.

This move to a "grand unification" is something that many projects are doing independently. Every week I encounter projects that take a little of Booch'91, some OMT, sprinkle it with Objectory or Shlaer/Mellor, maybe throw in a dash of structured analysis stuff for historical reasons, all in order to generate a method that's suitable to the particular culture and focus of that project or company. In my opinion, that's a good thing: if any of us methodologists had all the right answers as to the perfect way to develop every conceivable application, you wouldn't need to be reading anything else, nor would you ever have to worry about software development again, because tools could automate the whole process. This is obviously not going to happen in the near future, and so in the meantime, with real projects to get out the door and even more complex ones waiting in the wings, you have to be pragmatic and move forward with what works and what's proven. That in a very real sense is exactly what the Booch Method has evolved to.[14]

Will the method continue to evolve? Yes, as do all human artifacts. For instance, there is work to be done in learning how best to document application frameworks and how to approach the problems of enterprise-wide domain modeling. However, I anticipate a reasonably long period of stability, especially for the notation and core process. As Rumbaugh once observed to me, the process of evolutionary convergence will likely lead to standardization of object-oriented methods. The Booch Method is a major step in the direction of convergence and thus represents a waging of peace in the method wars.

NEXT GENERATION METHODS

The fastest-growing section of my professional library seems to be the part dealing with object-oriented technology. Rarely a month goes by that I don't add a new book that proposes yet another notation or process for object-oriented development. By my count, there are some 20 or so different object-oriented methods that purport to support the full development life cycle, countless variations on the theme of these basic methods, and a mul-

---

[14] [The industry's methods have matured since Grady wrote this article in 1994. I believe he would now recommend a project pick a well-defined, mature method, rather than growing its own. Consider the overhead that a grow-your-own project encounters, with respect to training, CASE tool support, etc. Also, unification is no longer a distant hope.]

titude of other partial life cycle development methods... and the number keeps growing at a steady pace. For the organization beginning to adopt the object-oriented paradigm, and even for the more experienced team trying to evolve to a more mature and well-defined development organization, this cacophony of notations is downright confusing. Method wars in such organizations are tantamount to the emotional language wars that are often waged in software development groups. C++ versus Smalltalk versus Eiffel versus Ada! Booch versus Rumbaugh versus Shlaer/Mellor versus Coad/ Yourdon! What is an organization to do? All too often, the battle cry is "let's create yet another notation and process!" Happily, most organizations (except for those with an attitude that their problem is so unique, or with more time and money on their hands than is healthy) quickly get over the idea of trying to create their own programming language.

Now, in general, I'm a fan of graphical notations. In this context, I like to quote the mathematician Alfred Whitehead who noted that "by relieving the brain of all unnecessary work, a good notation sets it free to concentrate on more advanced problems." Indeed, in practice, the use of an expressive yet simple notation can be greatly beneficial in crafting a complex object-oriented system. It is far too easy for the developer to cast adrift in a veritable sea of knotty tactical language details, and in so doing lose sight of a system's architecture. Notations can help us express analysis and design decisions at much higher levels of abstraction. Additionally, as Ralph Johnson, Bruce Anderson, Pete Coad, and Rebecca Wirfs-Brock have observed, well-structured object-oriented systems are full of patterns representing common collaborations of objects and classes. Indeed, one of the more interesting recent developments on the object-oriented scene has been their independent attempts to codify these patterns to form sort of an architectural handbook. Most interesting patterns transcend the design of individual classes, and a good notation can helps us visualize and reason about such patterns.

The development of notations for object-oriented technology seems to be paralleling the history of notations for structured analysis and design methods. In each field's infancy, there was at first a flurry of activity and opposing proposals as many different people explored the envelope of the problem space. Over time, as projects gained experience in using certain notations, and especially as tools developed to support such notations, there was a consolidation. Natural selection in the software development arena would tend to cast away all silly, inconsistent, or incomplete notations, and center upon those elements that added real value.

Object-oriented technology seems to have now matured beyond its awkward adolescent stage and entered the mainstream of industrial-strength software development. I have encountered the use of the object-oriented paradigm throughout the world, for such diverse domains as the administration of banking, insurance, and securities transactions, the automation of bowling alleys, cookie production, and semiconductor manufacturing, the management of public utilities, the control of pacemakers and other medical equipment, the operation of multinational command-and-control systems, and the mapping of the human genome. Many of the next-generation operating systems, database systems, telephone systems, avionics systems, and multimedia applications are being written using object-oriented techniques.

It is time for consolidation of notations. Stated even more strongly, at this stage of maturity, it is in the best interests of the software development community at large, and object-oriented technology in particular, for there to be standard notations for development. Standards can actually help to expand the marketplace, by providing a common language-independent vocabulary for developers to capture and then communicate their analysis and architectural decisions. Standard notations can facilitate the creation of tools as well, by encouraging the interchange of common development artifacts. Such standards also let tool builders focus their attention on more interesting issues than just what icons to draw, including issues such as forward- and reverse-engineering, semantic checks for consistency, constraints, and completeness, and the generation of metrics.

Over half a dozen formal- and semiformal method comparison papers have crossed my desk in the past year, and some interesting trends are emerging. Specifically, virtually all such comparisons have rated Booch and Rumbaugh as the "best" notations—by whatever criteria each comparison establishes—and most rate the expressiveness of these notations so close as to be statistically insignificant. Indeed, one large telephone company did two independent evaluations, one in the U.S. and one in Europe, and one report judged Booch as the "best" with Rumbaugh a close second, and the other judged Rumbaugh the "best" with Booch a close second. Go figure! This just points out that once core requirements have been satisfied, notational selection is often a matter of personal (or political) taste.

Rumbaugh's work is particularly interesting, for as even he and his co-authors observe, our methods are more similar than they are different. In addition to Jim's contributions to the field, I have surveyed the work of many other methodologists, interviewed projects that have applied their work, and where possible, tried their methods myself. Because I'm more interested in helping projects be successful with object-oriented technology than in dogmatically hanging on to practices solely for emotional or historical reasons, I've unilaterally tried to incorporate the best from each of these other methodologists, especially Rumbaugh, into my own method, with the purpose of trying to bring about notational unification.

Figuratively speaking, let's start with a clean sheet of paper and try to identify a core model that must be supported by any such comprehensive standard notation. Indeed, the important phrase here is "model," for that is what notations do: they serve to provide models for our analysis of the problem domain, as well as to provide models for the strategic and tactical decisions that form our software's architecture.

ANALYSIS

During *analysis*, we must address the following central questions:

- What is the desired behavior of the system?

- What are the roles and responsibilities of the objects that carry out this behavior?

Interestingly, the very focus of these questions is directly related to some recent work in the process of object-oriented analysis. As Jacobson and Goldberg discuss, the use of scenarios is a powerful way to elucidate the behavior of a system. In particular, Jacobson suggests a use-case approach to analysis, wherein the desired behavior of a system is expressed through a number of different scripts. In the context of Macintosh software development, Goldberg and Alger have expand upon this idea by distinguishing primary scenarios (ones that map to the system's function points) and secondary scenarios (ones that deal with second-order behavior, such as the system's responses to exceptional conditions). Goldberg and Rubin also note their focus upon behavior during analysis, and emphasize the different roles that objects play when collaborating to provide the system's behavior.

Notationally, these are all elements that cannot be expressed just by writing a set of C++ or Smalltalk classes. The behavior of individual objects, although interesting, is not sufficient, because the real behavior of a system derives from the collaborations among such objects. For this reason, in support of behavioral-based analysis, a standard notation must have some facility for capturing scenarios derived from use-case analysis, as well as some facility for representing the common roles and responsibilities among the classes whose objects provide this behavior.

In the Booch notation, we use object diagrams to show scenarios; this practice is virtually identical to object collaboration diagrams that other methodologists have proposed.[15] Rumbaugh suggests using textual scripts and data flow diagrams to capture these functional aspects of a system, but such models have proven difficult to integrate with the other products of his notation. Similarly, the original Booch notation lacked expressiveness in representing the dynamics of a scenario (users have reported that timing diagrams are unwieldy). However, combine the best of Booch and Rumbaugh, and you now have a simpler yet more expressive way to capture scenarios. Specifically, we retain the use of object diagrams from Booch, which let us indicate structural as well as functional collaborations among objects, and add Rumbaugh's practice of event traces—similar to Jacobson's practice of interaction diagrams, which serve as the scripts that animate these objects through their scenarios.[16]

Similarly, in the Booch notation, we use class diagrams to represent the common roles and responsibilities (as well as other relationships) among the classes whose objects provide this behavior. This is similar to Rumbaugh's

---

[15] [In UML, object diagrams will be called *collaboration* diagrams.]
[16] [In UML, these will be known as *sequence* diagrams.]

notation for his object model. However, the original Booch notation lacked support for associations, which—although semantically weak—have proven to be essential for analysis.[17] Similarly, Rumbaugh's notation lacks support for expressing certain strategic issues, most notably class categories (for dealing with clusters of classes),[18] as well as certain tactical issues, such as distinguishing plain and parameterized classes (essential to describing certain reusable patterns) and capturing decisions about object ownership and lifetimes (such as manifested in the C++ distinction of value versus reference versus pointer containment). Again, combine these best of Booch and Rumbaugh, plus add a way to capture the roles and responsibilities of abstractions, and you now have a self-consistent and expressive notation that can be applied to analysis as well as architectural and detailed design.

DESIGN

During *design*, we must address the following central questions relative to the system's architecture:

- What classes exist and how are those class related?

- What mechanisms are used to regulate how objects collaborate?

- Where should each class and object be declared?

- To what processor should a process be allocated, and for a given processor, how should its multiple processes be scheduled?

The first two elements relate to the logical architecture of a system, and are manifested in the unified class and object diagrams described earlier. The second two elements are manifested in module and process diagrams. These notational elements don't have a direct parallel in Rumbaugh, but in practice have proven to be important for expressing the physical architecture of a system, and essential to the creation of meaningful forward and reverse engineering tools.

---

[17] [In UML, the semantics of associations have tightened up greatly and are no longer semantically weak.]

[18] [In UML, a Booch category will be represented by a *package*.]

However, the original Booch notation was lacking in the expression of the dynamic semantics of these models. Specifically, there was support for state transition diagrams, but their use was not emphasized, and they lacked expressiveness. Rumbaugh and other methodologists have suggested the use of Harel's hierarchical state machines and so we have adopted this practice as well. Harel's work starts with simple state machines, and adds depth (the nesting of states), orthogonality (AND and OR combinations of states), and broadcasting (for the communication of events). As Coleman and others have observed, Harel's work has to be modified slightly to fit the object-oriented paradigm; in particular, broadcasting is generally not an appropriate mechanism, and explicit AND states are often better expressed as independent state machines for distinct objects. Rumbaugh didn't go all the way in adopting Harel's practice (in particular, he omits Harel's mechanism for history, whose presence can greatly simplify certain complicated state machines), but we have chosen to take what Rumbaugh included, and add the remaining interesting elements of Harel's work.

This leaves us with a grand unification of notations, in terms of the core concepts that it must encompass. Obviously, there are tactical issues that remain, including the shapes of particular icons, but even there, the notational differences are virtually entirely cosmetic. In unscientific surveys I've taken in my lectures the past year, a modest percentage prefer my cloud icon, about the same percentage prefer Rumbaugh's rectangles, but the overwhelming majority really doesn't care—as long as there are tools to support the notation.

To date, there are some seven commercially available tools that support the Booch notation, a smaller number that support Rumbaugh's notation, and many, many more individual tools that support home-grown notations. This is futile: I'd rather see an industry of developers and tool builders that support one notation, and that is indeed an explicit goal of this unification. In this manner, we can hope to leave the method wars behind us, and move on to the vastly more interesting issues of crafting software systems that add real value to this world.

UNIFICATION

I'm a rabid fan of "Star Trek." One of my favorite episodes from "The Next Generation" was entitled "Unification," whose main story line dealt with political unification (between the Vulcans and the Romulans), as well as unification of a more personal nature (spanning the eras of Kirk/Spock and Picard/Data). Albeit on a far less dramatic scale, there is a political, personal, and technical unification taking place in the world of object-oriented analysis and design. Because it has important implications for developers and toolsmiths, I want to explain the nature of this work, examine what it will mean to other methodologies, and offer some predictions for the next generation of object-oriented methods.

To explain the state of the object-oriented method world as it is today, I have to go back in time, in fact, I must return to over a decade ago. In the early 1980s, classic procedural languages such as COBOL, FORTRAN, and C dominated the scene. GUI-intense systems were still not quite in the mainstream, and personal computers were vastly underpowered and very much a novelty. Even at that time, however, there were developments in the background that, for those who were paying attention, telegraphed what was to come. Simula had come upon the landscape about a decade earlier in the late 1960s and had given rise in the 1970s to niche languages such as Smalltalk and various object-oriented flavors of Lisp. Ada was only beginning to take shape as was C++ (which made its first appearance in the early 1980s as C with Classes). Notwithstanding these evolutionary developments in languages, software development was still very much a labor-intensive event, involving teams of developers who would beat ever-growing bodies of code into submission. The notion of a development environment as we know it today was only then becoming understood. Software engineering itself was in transition, with methods such as Martin's Information Engineering, Jackson's Structured Design, and Yourdon and DeMarco's structured analysis and design (SA/DT) in the forefront, and with ideas about abstract data types only beginning to emerge from academia. It made sense that SA/DT techniques dominated, for they matched their problem domain (typically data-intensive, semi-interactive systems) and their languages (classical procedural languages) very well.

However, two things disturbed this delicate balance in the 1980s: the improving price/performance of personal computers, and the growing pervasiveness of networking. These two conditions made it possible to automate things to a degree never considered before. Even beyond the direct PC market, these two events had great impact, ultimately reshaping the entire software marketplace.

The early to mid-1980s marked the beginning of the first endeavors with analysis and design methods that broke from their structured past. I began writing about object-oriented design methods in 1983, and a few others, most notably Stephen Mellor, Peter Coad, and Jim Rumbaugh and his colleagues began to do the same. In 1988, Stephen and his colleague Sally Shlaer published their first book on object-oriented analysis (Shlaer & Mellor 1988). Shortly thereafter, a veritable flood of books on object-oriented analysis and design appeared, for example Booch (1991), Coad & Yourdon (1991), Martin & Odell (1992), Rumbaugh et al. (1991), and Jacobson et al. (1992). Now, there are two observations I'd like to make with regard to this infinite diversity of methods in infinite combinations (to borrow another Trek phrase): On the one hand, this publishing explosion was a good thing, because it represented a growth of experimentation in the object-oriented methods market. In short, different methodologists were approaching the same problem (solving hard software development problems) in a common way (using an object-oriented foundation) but from different perspectives (some more structural, others more behavioral; some more formal, others more casual). On the other hand, this deluge of methods was a bad thing, because it looked like there was no consensus in the market as to how to properly architect object-oriented systems. Especially for the first-time user of object-oriented stuff, the method wars were a serious distraction. I don't think that any one of us methodologists set out to wage war: it just naturally happened that way as our different approaches faced one another in the real world.

Happily, the real world has a wonderful built in mechanism for stability: Those ideas that work tend to survive, and those that do not work as well tend to fade away. In the late 1980s and early 1990s, that's exactly what began to happen. As real projects used these methods across a variety of problem domains, it became clear what modeling issues were important (such as the importance of modeling collaborations of objects) and which were not (such as the use of data-flow diagrams to show functionality). Thus, natural selection set in, forcing methodologists to adapt or die, so to speak. In the early 1990s we saw evolution among the major methods, most notably Booch (who began to adopt elements from OMT), Rumbaugh (who began to adopt elements from Booch), Mellor, and Coad. Coming from a different direction was Ivar Jacobson, who brought to the table his idea of use-case-based analysis. As it turns out, his concepts proved very useful in practice and therefore stuck, and in fact were grafted onto most of the other mainline methods. Simultaneously, there emerged a symbiotic relationship with the tool vendors, who at first tended to produce tools that supported every imaginable method (and then some), but then that settled down to mainline support for just a few methods (largely because developers were beginning to self-choose methods in the market).

Now, I'll be the first to admit that there was distinct rivalry amongst us methodologists in the late 1980s and early 1990s. To a large degree, we each felt we had the "right" approach. I suppose it was an entirely human response, and one can find parallels in any number of similar scientific ventures (such as the debate over AC versus DC power distribution in the late 1800s, or VHS versus Betamax in the 1970s). However, in the early 1990s, a technical and then a personal unification among some of the methods and methodologists began to take place. As I mentioned, revisions of my early work adopted ideas from Jim Rumbaugh (and others); similarly revisions of his work adopted ideas from me (and others). Both of us adopted use-case concepts from Ivar.

That is why it made a great deal of sense for Jim and I to join forces as we did in late 1994. At that time, we set out to truly unify our methods by forming a single, common notation and process because it was clear that we were already independently moving in that direction and that the market desired such a unification. Our critics expected we would fail. Jim and I were optimistically cautious. It did take a good deal of hard work, but we achieved what we set out to do, namely, the fusion of OMT and Booch.

As I also mentioned, both Jim and I had independently adopted Ivar Jacobson's use-case ideas, and thus it made great sense that Ivar join us formally as well. He did so in late 1995, and since that time, we three have been working to fuse our work into one. At is turns out, Jim and I had already made a good effort at incorporating Ivar's ideas into our unification, but with Ivar close at hand, we are now able to go all the way.

The path we are on will lead us to formal standardization some time in early 1997. Our focus has first been upon the standardization of notation, not process, because a notation shapes the artifacts that every project uses. Furthermore, a single, common notation is amenable to a variety of processes.

We have been very open about our work and so have actively sought public feedback. We have also explicitly invited any tool vendor who was interested to get early and ongoing information about our work, so as to enable widespread support for the unified modeling language (UML). We realize that we have a unique opportunity to put a stake in the ground with regard to industrial-strength object-oriented methods. Since we have effectively one last shot to get this right, and since we expect that this method will be relatively long-lived, we are being very deliberate about our work, trying to validate what we've done by applying it to use cases from a variety of real modeling problems.

This work will reach closure sometime in early 1997. That doesn't mean I'll be looking for a new job or anything, but it does mean that we will have reached a point of stability in the domain of object-oriented methods. As I'll explain in a moment, however, methods must continue to evolve, because the rules of software development continue to evolve.

What does this mean for other methodologies? The best analogy I can offer is this: At various times, the trade press has reported that language X was going to totally dominate all others.[19] At the same time, it was feared that

---

[19] Choose your favorite language: C, Ada, Smalltalk, C++, CLOS, Objective-C, Visual Basic, or even Java.

if any one language dominated, then all interesting future developments in language research would be locked out. This has never happened. Indeed, certain languages have dominated a particular region for a time, but there has always been a place for a variety of alternatives.

So it is among object-oriented methods. By all accounts I've read, the use of Booch plus Objectory plus OMT already represents a majority among developers who use object-oriented methods, and so I expect this will remain true of the UML as well. The UML is indeed the legitimate successor to all three of these methods. Other methods will continue to survive as long as they add value and are perceived as offering some advantage for some particular domain. Over time, I expect some of these lesser used methods to either fade away, or be consolidated with others. Notwithstanding this natural selection process, innovations will continue to be made, and where it makes sense, we will try to incorporate them into the UML. Our challenge is thus to form an expressive method, yet one that is simple enough that it does not become the PL/1 of methods.[20]

I must point out that what we are doing in the UML is far more than simply consolidating the Booch, Objectory, and OMT methods. Consolidation is certainly our first step, but we've gone beyond basic unification and have tried to address more advanced modeling issues. Thus, we've added features such as stereotypes and properties, which collapse a number of previously orthogonal features into one as well as offer a means of extensibility. Furthermore, we've found ways to address distribution and migration, as well as to express other views of a system's architecture.

It's utterly impossible to predict the future of software development, but it is clear that the rules seem to keep changing at a very rapid pace. The first wave of software development was centered around building modest-sized monolithic systems. The second wave centered around building very large-sized monolithic systems. The third wave centered around modest-sized component-oriented systems. The current way, as typified by the Java style

---

[20] For those not familiar with PL/1, this is a language that's a curious mixture of features from COBOL, FORTRAN, and lots of other procedural languages, forming a distinctly inharmonious whole.

of applets, or the Microsoft OLE/COM style of componentware, or the OMG CORBA style of distributed computing, centers around very large-size component-oriented systems. Speaking of the rapid pace, note that these four waves all happened over a period of only about twenty years.

Development environments are much more common today than they were just a few years ago, and frameworks, application builders, and 4GLs have helped to eliminate some of the tedium. One factor remains the same across all these waves of development, and that's the fact that successful software development is still a very hard thing, and requires a lot of hard effort. Market forces are such that development organizations will always be compelled to push the envelop of what is possible. From a methodological perspective, it's important to realize that most organizations worldwide still don't follow any mature, repeatable method. Thus, although the Booch/Objectory/OMT methods may be the most commonly used method among object-oriented developers who use methods, the fact is that the larger majority are not using any method at all. This represents an opportunity, for it means that there are many who could benefit from a standard method. Happily, I'm encouraged by the signs that I see. As I go about the world, I encounter more and more people who have the title "architect" on their business cards (although what "architect" means varies widely from person to person). I also encounter more and more organizations serious about instituting a mature development process. (This is partly motivated by the SEI CMM and the dictates of ISO 9000, but mostly motivated by the growing recognition that mature development processes are sound economic business.)

This is precisely the environment we have in mind for the future of UML. We expect coming systems to be far more distributed and component-oriented, and that most organizations will want to focus on architecture-driven incremental and iterative processes. We've tried to reflect these needs by providing the right modeling features in the Language. For that reason, we expect that the UML will represent a stable modeling language of choice for many over the next multiple years. That's good news for developers, because it means they can benefit from its maturity. That also means that Jim, Ivar, and I still have a lot to do, because users will continue to push the UML in ways we could never anticipate. By working in this small team, we expect we will be able to adapt the UML as needed, yet keep it conceptually simple. This does not mean that you will see the UML changing wildly. Rather, we recognize that we must stabilize it this year, and allow only simple evolutionary changes, just as happens in the world of programming languages.

QUALITY SOFTWARE AND THE UNIFIED MODELING LANGUAGE

Worldwide, there is an insatiable demand for software. On the one hand, that's great news. These are exciting times for the professional software developer, for this is still largely an era of innocence and unbounded opportunity. On the other hand, that's the worst possible news. No amount of heroic programming will ever suffice to meet this demand. Furthermore, as software continues to weave itself deeply into the fabric of society, the stakes have gotten higher. Unfortunately, software bugs are still considered just a normal part of the territory, but now, they may manifest themselves in the fall of a business or even worse, in the loss of a human life.

In addition to this insatiable demand is the almost rabid rate of change in software development technology. Eighteen months on the calendar is an eon in software years. Blink and you will miss the next great shift. Just a year ago, C++ was hot. These days, it's Java and Visual Basic. Middleware such as OLE and CORBA, visual programming, and component-based programming have changed the rules. The great operating system wars still rage on. Frankly, I've given up predicting what might come next.

Although I refuse to predict technological change, I can safely predict the future of software: it's going to be more complex and it's going to be far more distributed. It's going to be far more complex mainly because of demand-pull and supply-push, to use an economic analogy. User expectations for what software can do are exceedingly high. Furthermore, what is possible is far greater now than just a few years ago. The cost of computing has plummeted, yet the cost and complexity of software development have continued to increase. Future systems will be far more distributed for similar reasons. The economics of networking are such that, in the future, the network will be the computer. Additionally, the partly technical, partly social phenomenon of the Web has fueled the drive toward pervasive distribution.

Despite all of the excitement and the rhetoric, one thing does remain constant: Building complex software of quality and of scale is still fundamentally a hard problem. Simply put, this means that—all the latest technology trends notwithstanding—deploying quality software is still an engineering problem. As for any engineering problem, this implies striking a balance between artistry—for the best software is often a thing of beauty—and science.

On the science side, my experience suggests that there are a number of best practices found in common among projects that are successful. Two of those practices that stand out are a focus on architecture, and a focus on an iterative and incremental development process.

A focus on architecture means not just writing great classes and algorithms, but also crafting simple and expressive collaborations of those classes and algorithms. All quality systems seem to be full of these kinds of collaborations, and ongoing work in the area of software patterns is beginning to name and classify them so that they can more easily be reused (Gamma et al. 1995). The best architectures I find have, as Fred Books calls it, "conceptual integrity," and that derives from the project's focus on exploiting these patterns and making them simple, which turns out to be very hard to do.

An iterative and incremental development process reflects the rhythm of the project. *Projects in crisis have no rhythm,* for they tend to be opportunistic and reactive in their work. *Successful projects have a rhythm,* reflected in a regular release process that tends to focus on the successive refinement of the system's architecture. This is what Microsoft calls "synch and stabilize," and it's a practice which brings results, for systems of just about any complexity.

A focus on architecture and a focus on process may appear to be simple enough things for a project to institute. In the heat of battle, however, when an unstoppable deadline comes rushing at you, the easy thing to do is abandon these practices. I got into a discussion with a programmer recently, who told me of her company's shift to the use of C++. I asked if they were using any object-oriented analysis and design techniques, and she replied that they didn't have time for that. I then asked her if they were meeting their schedules and target metrics. She said, with some embarrassment, no. Suddenly, I had a Dilbert moment: The cause and effect were just so evident to me, and yet, head down, worrying about the daily blocking and tackling of her project, she just didn't see the connection.

This is not an isolated incident. Some of you may have heard me talk about a couple of horror stories:

> This particular project in crisis had written several hundred thousands of lines of C++. A quick review revealed that the team had written lots of code, but not one single class.

> Another project was similarly in crisis. A quick review here revealed that the team had written hundreds of thousands of lines of C++, and that they had about the expected number of classes for that size system. However, further investigation revealed that, on the average, each class had about one member function, usually named with some variation of the phrase "do it."

I'm not saying that these projects were clueless, but they both did ignore a pretty fundamental principle: *quality software doesn't happen; rather, it's engineered that way.*

This is where object-oriented methods come in. I've been living with this technology since the early 1980s. In the years following—characteristic of almost every emerging discipline—there was an explosion of object-oriented methods as various methodologists experimented with different approaches to object-oriented analysis and design. Experience with a number of these methods grew, accompanied by a growing maturation of the field as a whole as more and more projects applied these ideas to the development of production quality, mission-critical systems. Initially, a few methods began to take root, having added value to a number of projects. These methods included ones such as Booch, OMT, Shlaer/Mellor, Odell/ Martin, RDD, OBA, and Objectory. By the mid-1990s, a few second-generation methods began to appear, most notably Booch'94, the continued evolution of OMT, and Fusion. By this time, object orientation was decidedly in the mainstream. The important thing about all of these methods is that they attempted to bring about a balance of artistry and science to complex software development.

Given that the Booch and OMT methods were already independently growing together and were collectively recognized as the dominant object-oriented methods worldwide, Jim Rumbaugh and I joined forces in October 1994 to forge a complete unification of our work. Both Booch and OMT had begun to adopt Ivar Jacobson's use cases, and thus it was natural that in the Fall of 1995, Ivar formally joined this unification effort.

Currently, we are focused on what we call the Unified Modeling Language. UML is a third-generation method for specifying, visualizing, and documenting the artifacts of an object-oriented system under development. UML represents the unification of the Booch, Objectory, and OMT methods, and additionally incorporates ideas from a number of other methodologists, most notably Wirfs-Brock, Ward, Cunningham, Rubin, Harel, Gamma, Vlissides, Helm, Johnson, Meyer, Odell, Embley, Coleman, Coad, Yourdon, Shlaer, and Mellor. UML is the direct and upwardly compatible successor to the Booch, Objectory, and OMT methods. By unifying these three leading object-oriented methods, UML provides the basis for a common, stable, and expressive object-oriented development method.

Although the UML itself is intentionally quiet on process, one process that UML must enable is one that is use-case driven, architecture-centric, and both incremental and iterative. In many ways, UML tries to codify the best practices that we and others have encountered in successful object-oriented projects worldwide. Thus, also in many ways, we are not really the "inventors" of anything radically new. Rather, the value that UML brings is that we've observed what works and what doesn't in the world of object-oriented software development, and tried to package that up in the form of a modeling language that scales to systems of complexity.

I have no expectations that the fundamental problems of software development will go away in my lifetime. However, what I do know is that a continued engineering focus will help mitigate those problems, and development such as the UML are one stake in the ground helping to define that engineering focus.

SCENARIOS

Today's newspaper was filled with advertisements for the latest blockbuster movies. There were the usual offerings, some light romantic comedies, a few action/adventure pictures (distinguishable by varying numbers of explosions per minute), and as is typical for this time of the year, one or two legal thrillers. Having just finished an engagement helping a software client architect an application, I was suddenly struck by the similarities between the process of crafting movies and the process of crafting software. Both require a fair amount of creativity. Both must apply this creativity in the context of a very technical foundation. Both involve the delivery of tangible products under demanding schedules. Finally, both entail problems whose requirements are rarely, if ever, complete, correct, unambiguous, and never-changing.

There is another part of the process of making movies that has proven to be quite useful in the business of writing software, and that part is storyboarding.

First, some history. The Booch Method as it was defined in 1990 was admittedly weak with regard to analysis. In defense, I would have to say that at that time there was simply not enough good experience with any of the various object-oriented analysis approaches to warrant declaring that one approach was better than the other. Furthermore, the reality of transitioning organizations from structured approaches to object-oriented stuff created some pressure to maintain a path from the traditional techniques of data-flow diagramming to an object-oriented solution.

The world has changed a great deal since 1990. As experience with OMT has shown, trying to integrate data-flow diagrams with purely object-oriented models just doesn't work very well. Jim Rumbaugh has agreed with this observation. Although the data-flow approach may appeal to the experience of developers schooled in structured analysis techniques, trying to reconcile processes and data flows with classes and objects often requires more than a little magic. On the other hand, Jacobson's work on use cases has proven to be quite effective for capturing and then analyzing requirements (Jacobson et al. 1992, and Jacobson et al. 1994). Couple this with the activity of business process reengineering, and use cases turn out to be a very powerful means of communication among domain experts, users, and developers concerning the desired behavior of a system.

This is why I chose to adopt Jacobson's use-case concept. This is also why—in the spirit of waging peace in the object-oriented method wars—I chose to directly adopt Jacobson's notation for interaction diagrams, his representation for use cases instances. Let me assure you, however, that I did not just tack interaction diagrams on to the front of my earlier work and leave them dangling there as an unintegrated piece. Interaction diagrams have an important role to play in the Booch Method with regard to requirements discovery, architecture, testing, and traceability.

Let's return to the problem of movie-making. In very simple terms, the process of producing a movie begins with some statement of the picture's story, characters, and scenes. Once the basic shape of the movie is agreed upon (in a sense, when the requirements of the movie are established by the production company), then planning continues with the creation of a script.

Because the flow of a movie is so important, storyboards are commonly used to elaborate upon the picture's action. Storyboarding, actually a part of movie-making since its beginnings, emerged as a fundamental practice through the efforts of Walt Disney and other animators during the 1930s. Today, the use of storyboarding is pervasive and has even received a further boost through the presence of a number of PC-based tools that help automate the storyboarding process.

Specifically, a storyboard "provides the continuity of the action, which is worked out scene by scene simultaneously with the ... script. In the storyboard, the story is told and to some extent graphically styled in a succession of key sketches with captions and fragments of dialogue."[21] A storyboard thus represents a path through the flow of the movie, in other words, a scenario that can be played back.

Storyboards serve three purposes. First, they provide a means of capturing decisions about the action in the movie. Depending upon the nature of a particular scene, a storyboard might be very detailed (in other words, high-fidelity, perhaps even showing camera angles and background action), or it might be very coarse (that is, low-fidelity, showing only the placement of a few key characters). Second, they provide a vehicle for communicating these decisions to all the various parties in the production company, and letting them discuss and reason about the meaning or the details of a particular scene. Finally, they serve as instructions to the director, who is responsible for taking a script and its associated storyboards and implementing it through concrete camera work.

And so it is with software development. A scenario (or a use case, if you prefer Objectory's terminology) provides an outline of activities that signifies some system behavior. Scenarios document decisions about requirements or designs, provide a focus for communication about a system's semantics, and can serve as a blueprint for detailed implementation.[22]

For example, consider a decision-support system for managing consumer loans. End users probably have a number of scenarios that they view as central to this business domain, such as:
- Applying for a loan
- Making a payment on a loan
- Paying off a loan

---

[21] Motion Pictures. (1985). Britannica 15th ed. vol. 24, p. 438.

[22] [You've probably noticed by now that Grady used the terms use case and scenario almost interchangeably. I'm sure that since the publication of this article in 1994, Ivar Jacobson and he have had long talks about the differences. In the object community, there still remains a difference of opinion whether a scenario should be defined by a logically single thread or not. UML actually views this as more of a process issue than a notation issue.]

- Checking the history of payments on a loan
- Selling the loan to another financial institution
- Handling a late or a missed loan payment

A rule of thumb suggests that even the most complex application can be characterized in terms of a few dozen *primary scenarios*. This is true even in domains as sophisticated as telephone network services or in air-traffic control. In each case, there typically are only a modest number of primary scenarios that model the central problem. The operative word here is *primary*, a term suggested by Goldstein and Alger (Goldstein & Alger 1992). (Objectory/OOSE has a related concept, in which we distinguish uses cases that represent basic courses and alternative courses.) Basically, a primary scenario represents some fundamental system function. For example, a primary scenario of a telephony system would involve making a connection from one telephone to another. In an air-traffic control system, the scenario of an aircraft entering a controlled airspace would represent a primary behavior.

Of course, even the smallest system involves a multitude of possible exceptional conditions and alternative paths. Goldstein and Alger call these *secondary scenarios*, not because they are of secondary importance, but mainly because each secondary scenario typically represents some variation on the theme of a primary scenario. Thus, primary and secondary scenarios often form a hierarchy: a secondary scenario is often *"a kind of"* a primary scenario, with variations.[23]

Thus, as viewed from the outside by its end users and domain experts, the entire desired behavior of a software system can be captured through a web of scenarios, in much the same way as a storyboard does in making a movie. However, the analogy between the process of software development and the process of movie making breaks down because of the mention of the word *web*. Movies —at least, with today's technology—have only one path of action through them, and so can generally be represented by one long, continuous storyboard. All interesting software applications rarely if ever have a single path of behavior. Rather, the behavior of most complex applications,

---

[23] [These are sometimes modeled in Objectory/OOSE as uses and extends relationships between use cases, but not with a specialization (inheritance) relationship.]

114

especially those driven by external events including user interaction, are best characterized by a set of nearly-independent scenarios.

I've borrowed Simon's terminology here (Simon 1982). Scenarios are *nearly independent* in the sense that they can be studied in isolation, although in reality each one has some semantic connection to other scenarios. For example, a scenario exposing the activity of making a payment on a loan can be discussed with end users and developers in isolation. Furthermore, the scenario for paying on a loan interacts with the scenario for checking the loan history (payment is an important historical event in the lifetime of a loan) as well as with the scenario for handling a late payment (the record of past payments has a bearing on the course of action; one missed payment by a valued customer might result in sending a polite letter, whereas a late payment by an habitually late customer might result in a more personal visit).

In the context of an object-oriented system, scenarios provide a means of elaborating upon the behavior that results from the collaboration of several classes or objects. Just as scenarios rarely stand alone, classes and objects also rarely stand alone in a complex system, but rather, collaborate among themselves. For example, in a telephone system, the primary scenario of making a phone call involves at a minimum the collaboration of four agents: two terminals (in other words, the individual telephones), a path (representing a physical path through the network), and a conversation (a conceptual object, representing the telephone connection itself; conversations are important because each one represents something the telephone company can bill customers for). Several secondary scenarios might be used to represent variations upon this theme. For example, what should happen if the physical path goes down? What should happen if, while trying to make a connection, we find that the calling party has no authorization to call the given number, perhaps because the customer has blocked all outgoing long-distance calls for that line? In each case, these secondary scenarios involve the same core objects as in their common primary scenario.

Thus, it is fair to say that, in object-oriented systems, most interesting scenarios cut across large parts of the architecture, each one touching a different set of collaborating classes or objects. Indeed, the most interesting and elegant abstractions are typically those that participate in many such scenarios.

For example, in a number of windowing systems, the class View (or whatever it might be named) often participates in several scenarios: rendering objects on the screen, collaborating with the desktop manager during resizing and iconification, and synchronizing with other views of the same model. In fact, in most well-structured object-oriented systems, the development team will have distributed responsibilities such that no class or object participates in only one scenario, and such that each scenario involves a small number of classes or objects.

What good are scenarios in object-oriented software development? In my experience, scenarios, much like storyboards in movie-making, serve three main purposes:

- Scenarios are an essential part of capturing the requirements about a system. Scenarios speak the language of the end user and domain expert, and thus provide a way for them to state their expectations about the desired behavior of a system to its developers. Scenarios can be either low-fidelity or high-fidelity, depending upon the relative importance of the details to its end users. For example, in the early stages of analysis of an inventory control system, it might be sufficient to explain the scenario of taking an item out of a warehouse in just a few free-form sentences. On the other hand, in a human-critical system such as in a flight-control system, it might be necessary to spell out details such as timing and presentation, perhaps even showing prototype screens.

- Scenarios provide a vehicle for communication. By focusing end users and domain experts upon scenarios at the level of the problem domain, it helps them avoid the temptation of diving into solution-oriented abstractions. By focusing developers upon scenarios, it forces them to be grounded in the language of the problem domain, and also forces them to consider an intelligent distribution of responsibilities throughout the system. Scenarios, no matter what representation they might take, also address the social aspect of joint development, by providing a common artifact that users and developers can talk about, cast stones at, mark up in joint discussions, and ultimately evolve.

- As the project advances, scenarios serve as instructions to individual developers as well as to the testing team. For the developer, each scenario provides a reasonably unambiguous statement of the system's desired behavior, which must be satisfied by the collection of classes and objects presently under development. For the testing team, a scenario provides a reasonably unambiguous statement of testable behavior, first established as a system requirement and ultimately realized by the products of the developer. In this manner, there is an obvious kind of traceability possible, from the scenarios that capture system requirements, through the classes and objects that collaborate to provide this behavior, to the system tests that serve to verify that the system properly carries out this behavior.

What are scenarios not good for in object-oriented software development? In practice, scenarios turn out to be a marvelous way to characterize and then validate the resulting object-oriented architecture. However, it is important to realize that *scenarios do not by themselves define an architecture.* Every well-structured object-oriented architecture consists of at least two elements: a static dimension, consisting of a sea of classes arranged in hierarchies, and a dynamic dimension, consisting of a set of mechanisms that define the temporal collaborations among certain classes and objects. Scenarios, as expressed in interaction diagrams or in object diagrams, are useful for communicating this dynamic dimension. Furthermore, as an architecture evolves, it can be validated by running it against various new scenarios. From the outside, either as a paper exercise or in the context of an executing prototype, the team might apply different scenarios against the system and see how it then must be adapted to accommodate this new behavior.

What form do scenarios take? As I have alluded to, scenarios manifest themselves in a number of different ways. In the Booch Method, I suggest the use of three different concrete representations: CRC cards, interaction diagrams, and object diagrams.

[Editor's note: In UML, responsibilities are first-class citizens and the underlying semantics can be represented. Interaction diagrams, also known as an OMT event trace, are now called *sequence diagrams,* because they primarily represent a temporal flow of interactions. Object diagrams are renamed *collaboration diagrams*, because they show the dynamic linkages between objects in the system. In the remainder of this article, the UML terminology replaces the original Booch terminology.]

First, CRC cards prove to be a delightful way to brainstorm about scenarios. CRC cards are sort of the poor man's CASE tool, requiring a trivial investment of a few dozen index cards and some pencils with really good erasers. Their major attractions as a serious development technique are that they are totally free-form, they encourage the active participation by the development team, and they force the team to consider the intelligent distribution of responsibilities throughout the architecture. In practice, I have found CRC cards to be most useful early in the life cycle, at which time a system's requirements are the most fuzzy, and equally useful during design, particularly when exploring the dark corners of some aspect of the architecture. Elaborating upon a scenario with CRC cards also turns out to be a good way to identify the abstractionists on your team; they are the people who tend to end up in the center of a CRC card exercise.

However, CRC cards do suffer from one major limitation: after elaborating upon a scenario, you can't just wrap a rubber band around your pack of cards, hand them to the customer, and declare victory. CRC cards are inherently very dynamic beasts, and left by themselves, don't communicate the temporal aspects of a scenario.

Sequence diagrams, such as the one shown in figure 2, mitigate the problems associated with CRC cards. In fact, in practice, I often start with CRC cards for brainstorming, then, as the semantics of my scenario become more concrete, capture the flow of the scenario in a sequence diagram.

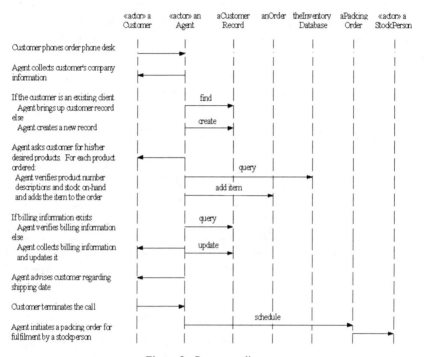

Figure 2. Sequence diagram.

The major attraction of sequence diagrams is that they clearly show the flow of activity in time, stating at the top of the script and running down the diagram. Sequence diagrams are especially well-suited for communicating business processes, because at a high level, they speak the language of end users and domain experts. Thus, early in the life cycle, we would use sequence diagrams that contain message flows written with free-form text. As we continue to evolve the architecture and establish various implementation details, we might show the same diagram, but now with concrete operations written for each message flow. In this manner, each sequence diagram (which expresses some temporal aspect of the system) achieves a tight coupling with the system's class diagrams and state transition diagrams (which collectively express some atemporal aspect of the system).[24]

Sequence diagrams suffer from one limitation: they can only show collaborative activity that is relatively sequential in nature. Sequence diagrams cannot by themselves show concurrent messaging, timing considerations, or more spatial issues, such as the fact that one object in the diagram is actually an attribute of another.

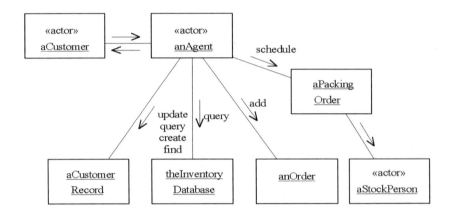

Figure 3. Collaboration diagram.

Collaboration diagrams, such as the one shown in figure 3, mitigate the problems associated with sequence diagrams. In a very real sense, sequence diagrams and collaboration diagrams are isomorphic. In other words, to some level of detail, it is possible to transform a sequence diagram into a collaboration diagram, and vice versa. Thus, sequence diagrams and collaboration diagrams can be viewed as alternative representations of the same scenario.

In practice, I tend to use sequence diagrams for capturing decisions about threads through the system, especially those sequential activities that end users see in any number of management information systems. For all other

---

[24] [As mentioned previously, there is some debate in the industry whether a scenario, (e.g. represented on a sequence diagram,) should represent only one logical thread through the system or not. Feedback on the UML 0.8 draft indicated a strong demand to allow branching and recursion for practical needs, so notation for these has been added. A given development process may enforce a single-thread constraint, of course.]

cases, where flow of control is not so strongly sequential, I prefer collaboration diagrams. For some developers, it ultimately ends up being a matter of taste, and a matter of how much additional detail (such as concurrency semantics and attributes) that must be shown to explain the scenario.

Where do scenarios fit in the software development process? In very general terms, scenarios show up in a number of stages of development. Very early in the life cycle, I recommend that the team start simply by enumerating the primary scenarios that characterize the system. This process forces the drawing of a boundary around the system. As requirements analysis unfolds, these scenarios are elaborated, and secondary scenarios are discovered. Herein, I use the following rule of thumb: At such time the team elaborates about 80% of the primary scenarios and a few of the interesting and representative secondary scenarios, then it is desirable to proceed on to architectural design. Do much more, and you reach diminishing returns. Do any less, and you run the risk of not knowing enough about the problem being solved to meaningfully move forward. Tangibly, these scenarios can be documented, delivered, and approved as a set of sequence diagrams and/ or collaboration diagrams.

As architectural design proceeds, additional scenarios are elaborated, both to validate the architecture and to document tactical mechanisms of the implementation. As earlier, these scenarios are documented in the form of sequence diagrams and/or collaboration diagrams, to serve as lasting artifacts of the architecture, and to be used by the testing team for subsystem testing. As we evolve this architecture in an incremental and iterative manner, we use these existing scenarios to verify that we have not regressed. The team also adds new scenarios to drive the process of evolving the architecture to new levels of functionality.

Toward the end of the project, we must realistically throw away some of these scenarios, because no project can afford to maintain every artifact that we used as scaffolding during development. Ultimately, our project must leave behind only those scenarios necessary to record the system's requirements, as well as those that record key architectural decisions. Retain any more, and you run the risk of drowning the system's maintainers in a sea of needless detail. Retain any less, and you make future consistent evolution of the system difficult, if not outright impossible.

In all fairness, I must admit that there is a dark side to scenario-based development. By focusing upon scenarios during requirements capture, you run the very real risk of analysis paralysis, mainly because it is so easy for the team to get wrapped up in a flood of details, particularly when considering exceptional conditions. If you find your team agonizing over the details of a few scenarios and never seeming able to break loose, then your project is surely in danger of thrashing. Usually, you can break this logjam in one of two ways: lock the responsible people in a room and don't let them leave for any reason until they get agreement, or apply the Nike philosophy of software development—*"Just do it"*—and call for the creation of a rapidly developed prototype.

Another very real danger is that your development team will take these object-oriented scenarios and turn them into a very nonobject-oriented implementation. In more than one case, I've seen a project start with scenarios, only to end up with a functional architecture, because they treated each scenario independently, creating code for each thread of control represented by each scenario. Usually, you can mitigate this problem by forcing reviews of the architecture as it evolves.

Used wisely, scenarios are an extremely effective way to clarify requirements, design, and desired implementation.

PROPERTIES AND STEREOTYPES

In formulating our unification, Jim and I first focused upon the construction of an underlying metamodel, which allowed us to come to fairly rapid agreement upon the semantics of the fundamental modeling concepts necessary to address the analysis, design, and construction of complex systems. In the process of this work, we found the need to introduce two elements that were new to Booch and OMT, yet which generalized some disparate concepts that had appeared in somewhat inconsistent ways in both Booch and OMT. We also found that these features offered us a means of making the notation extensible without change to its underlying semantics. These two elements include *stereotypes*, a concept first proposed by Rebecca Wirfs-Brock, and *properties*, a concept familiar to Lisp programmers. In the rest of this article, I'll explain the evolution of these ideas, describe their semantics, and then offer some examples of how they may be used.

STEREOTYPES

Stereotypes offer a facility for metaclassification. In other words, a stereotype specifies the classification of one or more classes. Stereotypes are not metaclasses, however. A metaclass is the class of a class, and thus in Smalltalk, for example, each class has exactly one metaclass and each metaclass has exactly one instance.[25] In contrast, a given class may have zero or more stereotypes. Similarly, a stereotype may classify one or more classes.

If at first this seems confusing, it is really not: other methodologists have identified the need for this kind of metaclassification, starting with Wirfs-Brock. Ivar Jacobson uses a kind of metaclassification in Objectory, when he distinguishes among three kinds of objects: *interface*, *entity*, and *control*. These three kinds partition the class space into orthogonal groups. In Ivar's case, these groups are largely conceptual (that is, they have limited semantic impact) but they are important, because they offer useful mental and visual cues as to the use or intent of a particular object.

In the terminology of the UML, we would call each of Jacobson's three groups a *stereotype*. In this notation, we permit every class to have zero or more stereotypes, although we do not dictate what stereotypes exist.[26] In this manner, stereotypes are an extensible part of the notation: projects may

---

[25] Well, almost exactly. The class whose name is Metaclass is a little more complicated, since every metaclass is an instance of the class whose name is Metaclass. (This is not to be confused with the artist whose name was Prince, as this involves a whole different set of tangled relationships.)

[26] [The last time I spoke with Jim and Grady on this topic, there was ongoing debate here. If multiple stereotypes are allowed for a given class then the intent of the stereotype—to quickly convey stereotypical roles and responsibilities—may be lost. Stereotypes are also the prescribed solution for modeling certain fundamental entities, such as actors.]

define their own stereotypes that fit their style of development or particular domain.[27]

A classic example of the use of stereotypes involves the classification of exceptions. When developing with C++ or Smalltalk, it is common for a team to define (or reuse) a set of exception classes, which collectively capture common exceptional conditions. Most often, these exceptions will be presented as a hierarchy of classes, with each branch of this hierarchy denoting a different kind of exceptional condition. In this model, leaf classes represent concrete exceptional conditions, and intermediate classes represent more general conditions. In practice, none of these are "normal" classes: their only purpose is to reify these exceptional conditions. Furthermore, they are typically used only to throw or catch such conditions. Rarely will one make a *list* of exception objects, or pass an exception to another object to *manipulate* it (other than to catch it). Thus, from the perspective of the modeler, it is useful to distinguish these exception classes from all others. This distinction not only offers mental and visual cues, it can also be a hint to the underlying development environment that causes it to generate special semantic checks or even special boilerplate code.

In the UML notation, our metamodel allows every class to have zero or more stereotypes, where a stereotype is just a simple name in the scope of the project as a whole. Developers may specify a class' stereotypes graphically, as illustrated in figure 4, showing a simple hierarchy of exception classes drawn for the design of the C++ Booch Components:

---

[27] It is likely that we will predefine a number of commonly used stereotypes, however, so as to offer a basic set of classification primitives. This is not unlike the situation in the C++ standard, where a number of common classes are predefined (namely, the Standard Template Library, or STL for short).

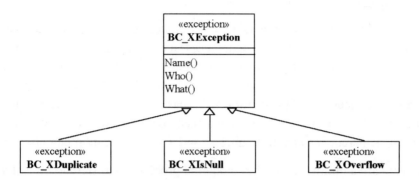

Figure 4. Class diagram showing exceptions as stereotypes.

Booch users will note that classes are rendered as rectangles. Yes, in the unified notation, the Booch cloud icon for classes has been replaced with the OMT-style rectangle. Although we wrestled with this issue for some time, it was clear this was the right decision: rectangles are easier to draw by hand and by tools, and moreover, they are far more space-efficient when a class is drawn with attributes and operations. Both Booch and OMT used a similar style for showing attributes and rectangles; thus, the only thing that really changes here in Booch is the shape of the class icon.

What is new to both Booch and OMT in the UML is how stereotypes are rendered. Specifically, the stereotypes of a class are listed above the class name, set off using guillemots («stereotype_name») which distinguish the stereotype from the class name.

One of the elements that is central to the unified notation is that we specify some idioms[28] for using the notation, and yet offer some explicit degrees of freedom for tool builders. For example, in tools and for printed diagrams, we recommend that class names be set apart from other elements of the class, by displaying the name in bold face. Similarly, we suggest that tools take advantage of the use of color to distinguish different stereotypes. For example, set by user preferences, a tool might render normal classes in black and white,

---

[28] Idioms have no semantic content; they are merely standard conventions for using the notation, set in place to preserve a common look and feel among uses of the notation.

while exception classes are rendered in red and white. Icons may also be used, such as a stick figure for an actor stereotype.

Returning to the underlying semantics of stereotypes, the careful reader might suggest that stereotypes are unnecessary, since the same effect can be obtained by using multiple inheritance. Let me be clear: stereotypes and multiple inheritance are quite distinct concepts. Stereotypes are largely a means of conceptual classification, whereas multiple inheritance implies type semantics: a stereotype is neither a class nor a type, whereas a class with multiple superclasses is both a subclass and a subtype of its superclasses.[29]

There are a multitude of other modeling problems that stereotypes solve. For example, in building event-driven systems, it is common to define a hierarchy of event classes similar in form to the hierarchy of exceptions classes that I introduced earlier. Just as for exceptions, events are not "normal" classes because they mainly serve to reify external (or internal) happenings and are thus used primarily in the context of state machines. One rarely manipulates an event object other than to acknowledge it or to respond to it. Thus, these event classes can best be mentally and visually distinguished by marking them as their own stereotype.

Although primarily conceptual in nature, stereotypes can be used as hints to back-end tools as to how to generate code. For example, in certain switching systems I've worked with, some classes may be marked as "extensible" meaning that their behavior (but not their interface) can be extended dynamically at run-time. From the application developers' viewpoint, these are just plain, ordinary classes, whose interfaces are well-defined and stable. From the system developers' viewpoint, however, these are extraordinary classes that participate in a special collaboration with the underlying run-time system. Specifically, if a class is marked as extensible, special code can be generated that causes objects of this class to register themselves with the runtime system and also to accept new state machines that specify their new behavior during their lifetime. By using stereotypes in this manner, projects

---

[29] The story on inheritance is a bit more complicated than this, since the UML reifies the concept of an interface, which permits the modeling of class and type hierarchies independently.

can define a language of their own that codifies common mechanisms in a concise manner.[30]

One last point. Stereotypes are adornments to basic class concepts, and as such are an advanced modeling element that can be ignored in all other situations. A class with no stereotypes specified is just a plain, ordinary class.

PROPERTIES

Closely related to the concept of stereotypes is the concept of *properties*. Whereas a stereotype is used to conceptually classify a class, a property is simply a name/value pair that may be attached to any element in the UML notation. This means that classes, objects, associations, operations, states, modules, and so on may all have a set of properties associated with them. A property is to a modeling element as an attribute is to a class.

Among other things, properties generalize a number of concepts in Booch that were originally treated as totally disparate. For example, Booch permitted adorning a class with the label *persistent* to identify it as "sticky" or as *active* to identify it as the root of a thread of control. In the unified notation, these concepts still exist, but they are treated as two possible properties of a class, namely, its persistence property (is it sticky or not) and its concurrency property (is it active or not).

A number of other elements in Booch collapse into the concept of properties. For example, Booch permitted a class to be marked as *abstract* by adorning it with a capital "A" inside an upside-down triangle. Experience has shown that, although this mark was visually distinctive, it was not space-efficient, and furthermore, it didn't translate well into other languages, especially those not using a Roman alphabet. Rather than treating abstract as an orthogonal element, it made sense for us to treat this as a property. As shown in figure 4 for the class BC_XException, we render properties by naming their value (or fully qualifying them by showing the entire name/value pair

---

[30] [One could say that in this example, we could have a property named "extensibility" in which the value extensible is particularly conceptually useful, so we also created a stereotype coincident with that value. If used for code generation, the stereotype value should probably also be the value of a clearly named property.]

in a list below the class name. Our hint to tool builders is that these properties be rendered in *italics* to set them apart visually.

As with stereotypes, we plan to include a number of predefined properties in the unified notation. In addition to the ones listed above, we expect to include properties such as *interface* (i.e. does this class reify a protocol, or is it a full class?) as well as pre- and post-conditions for individual operations.[31] To support the modeling of distributed systems, we expect to define a property, *location*, which can be used to specify the placement and movement of objects. Properties also help with regard to code generation. For example, we expect to specify a code-generation property for a number of modeling elements, so that developers can designate the idioms whereby modeling concepts are transmogrified into code. For example, such a code-generation property attached to an association might designate that a bag is used in 1-to-n relationships. Similarly, a code-generation property attached to one class might designate its target implement to be in Visual Basic, where the property of another class might target it to C++.

As for stereotypes, properties offer an escape clause in the UML. Projects (and tools) can define their own properties so as to codify elements that are important to their domain. For example, we imagine that projects might use properties to designate the author/owner of certain models, or to designate the phase (such as analysis or design) or release to which a particular element applies.

In summary, properties and stereotypes are found to be extremely useful. They elegantly solve many modeling problems, with minimal notation overhead.

---

[31] Pre- and post-conditions were part of Booch, but as with the concept of abstract classes, they appear as properties in the UML. We do not specify a language for pre- and post-conditions, but simply offer a place to put them. We view the semantics of conditions to be outside the scope of our work, and so leave their exact semantics to the domain of individual tools and projects.

FINITE STATE MACHINES

Reactive systems—that is, ones whose behavior is elicited in response to external events—are particularly well-suited to finite state machine modeling. There are in fact three reasons why this is so. First, finite state machines speak the language of the domain expert who often sees the world in terms of events and actions. Second, finite state machines have relatively straightforward and efficient mappings to code. Third, finite state machines are largely deterministic and so particularly amenable to rigorous analysis for conditions such as unreachable states and ambiguous transitions.

As illustrated in figure 5, the Booch Method uses Harel's notation for finite state machines, because it directly addresses the issues of scale and because it is already in fairly wide use outside the object-oriented world.[32]

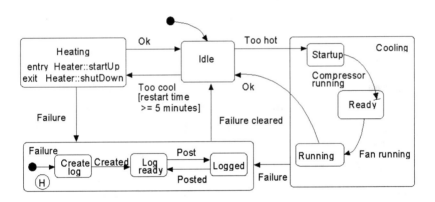

Figure 5. State diagram.

From the perspective of a domain expert in real time systems, one often views the world as a collection of finite state machines that operate concurrently. The object-oriented view of this world simply takes each relatively independent machine and encapsulates it inside an object. This object-ori-

---

[32] [UML will use almost identical notation.]

ented view offers the extra benefits of simplicity (the commonality among similar machines can be exploited in an inheritance lattice) as well as safety (the scope and behavior of each such machine is well-defined and is confined by class boundaries).

In the Booch Method, finite state machines may be associated with individual classes (although not every class requires an associated machine), with class categories, and with the system as a whole. These higher level machines typically represent the collection of the machines associated with objects at lower levels.

Using Harel's notation, finite state machines focus upon the following five entities:

Event — a circumstance to which the system may respond

Action — an operation that logically takes zero time

Activity — an operation that logically takes time

State — a named disposition of the system

Guard — a condition that protects a transition

Early in the development life cycle, it is appropriate to be imprecise in the meaning of these entities. However, as analysis and design proceed, their semantics become more and more important. At the limit, it is possible to generate executable code from precisely-defined finite state machines. Furthermore, with such precision, it is possible to employ tools that animate models of concurrent state machines and that analyze these cooperating machines for dangerous conditions.

In the Booch Method, these entities have the following semantics:

Event — a symbol that names a circumstance of interest to the system, or the name of an object that denotes such a circumstance

An event must be visible to any machine that wishes to respond to that event. Thus, external events that are of general interest must be defined globally; more local events such as ones representing internally generated circumstances can be declared in any enclosing scope for which there are machines that wish to respond to such events.

If events are just symbols, then typically any class whose objects must respond to an event will provide an operation that takes an event as a parameter and then acts to stimulates the underlying machine. If events are themselves objects, more sophisticated idioms are possible. For example, if we define the events in a system as a hierarchy of event classes, then we might pass about instances of a leaf class (which yields the idiom as for events as symbols) or we might pass about instances of intermediate classes (which so denote whole classes of events). In this latter idiom, we can rely upon the polymorphic behavior of event objects to trigger different behavior for specific kinds of events.

Continuing:

> *Action* — an operation within the scope of the enclosing state machine
>
> *Activity* — an operation within the scope of the enclosing state machine

Actions are typically attached to state transitions; they may also be triggered upon entering and exiting a state. Activities are typically associated with states, and so represent operations that continue while the object is in that particular state.

Actions and activities generally translate to operations local to the enclosing class (for example, a transition may trigger an operation upon the object that received the event) or they involve operations defined outside the class (for example, an event may trigger a service defined in a class utility).

States have similar scoping rules:

> *State* — a named disposition within the scope of the enclosing class or class category

In other words, states are local to individual classes. Two different classes may use the same state name, but these logically represent different states since they are elements of different machines. However, in the presence of inheritance, this also means that subclasses of a base class for which we have defined a finite state machine share same states. These subclasses may add their own new states and they may override the meaning of states defined in superclasses.[33]

Finally:

> *Guard* — an expression formed from objects and operations within the scope of the enclosing class or class category

In other words, a guard may involve any condition that can be calculated in the context of a given object. Guards are important because they provide a means of selectively ignoring events.

---

[33] The precise semantics of inheritance with finite state machines are quite complex. A few simplifying assumptions (such as limiting the scope of transitions to or from overridden states) help reduce the problem to one that is reasonably straightforward.

CHAPTER 6

ARCHITECTURE

Most individuals in the object technology industry think of Grady as a method-ologist, but I was fascinated to learn that Grady sees himself more as an architect. After all, the primary reason for using OO notation during software design and construction is to represent the desired or actual architecture. This has influenced Grady's perspective on notation, which is: given a desired architectural reality, what notation and semantic abstraction can best represent it? Grady's primary focus for OO models and processes has been to produce an effectively working architecture. Other OO methodologists have focused more on requirements or analysis. This diversity of focus has strengthened the industry. The combination of strengths evident in the UML is a good case in point.

Several excellent articles on architecture are included in this chapter:

- *The End of Objects and the Last Programmer*[1] describes the forces that drive society towards complexity and that drive the industry towards an OO approach. As the technology grows, so does its complexity. An architectural vision is essential to provide a structure for accommodating this complexity. Grady categorizes the various types of software architecture and describes their associated characteristics.

- *Conducting a Software Architecture Assessment*[2] addresses what the goals of a project assessment should be and what to look for during an assessment. He also presents an algorithm for conducting the assessment. In addition to architecture, Grady also discusses what to look for in assessing the team and its process.

---

[1] Based on the keynote address Grady delivered at the 1991 OOPLSA conference, the text of which was unpublished.

[2] Based on Booch, G. (1996). Conducting a software architecture assessment. *Object Magazine, 6*(4).

- In *Distributed Systems*[3] Grady presents several of the architectural issues that must be modeled. These include distribution, clustering, synchronization, interfaces, and migration. Readers with keen interest in these subjects are strongly encouraged to read the latest UML documents, because this area of the notation was still evolving when this book was published.

- *Patterns*[4] describes Grady's excitement over the patterns movement and presents pattern terminology. He describes the forms of patterns, their impact on architecture, and how they help the industry.

- *Patterns & Protocols*[5] discusses the implications of applying patterns to OO modeling and representing them in the UML. The relationships between patterns and protocols are discussed, with examples in the UML notation.

It is also worth mentioning some of Grady's other articles on the topic of architecture. In a section of *Coming of Age in an Object-Oriented World*,[6] Grady predicted how major layers of operating systems and application architecture infrastructures are evolving to an object-oriented form. He concluded with the insight: "From the perspective of the off-the-shelf software developer, this is an amazing trend: Virtually all the interesting standard interfaces for domain-specific functional elements will, over time, be cast in object-oriented forms. From the perspective of the custom software developer, this too is profound: Any frameworks that emerge from a custom development will have to exist in an object-oriented world." Grady also wrote several articles on the topic of architecture that were incorporated into Object Solutions.

---

[3] Based on Booch, G. (1995). Distributed systems. *Report on Object Analysis & Design, 2*(3).

[4] Based on Booch, G. (1993). Patterns. *Object Magazine, 3*(2).

[5] Based on Booch, G. (1996). Patterns and protocols. *Report on Object Analysis & Design, 2*(7).

[6] Booch, G. (1994). Coming of age in an object-oriented world. *IEEE Software, 11*(6).

THE END OF OBJECTS AND THE LAST PROGRAMMER

In 1989, Francis Fukuyama, a former deputy director of the U. S. State Department's Policy Planning Staff, wrote an article for *National Interest,* entitled "The End of History," in which he asserted that recent dramatic world events, including the dissolution of the USSR, represented a fundamental and final change in the evolution of governments. In 1992, he expanded upon this article in his book *The End of History and the Last Man.*[7] His observations regarding the state of global affairs and the role of the individual in such matters have a intriguing parallel to the growth and maturation of object-oriented technology.

Consider for a moment Fukuyama's premises. He suggests that there are two motors of history that drive the evolution of all social institutions. First, there is the *logic and direction of modern science.* Scientific inquiry is a rational process whose resulting knowledge is cumulative and, ultimately, irreversible. Although some knowledge may be "lost," the underlying truths upon which this knowledge is founded persist, leading to their eventual "rediscovery." The fruits of science greatly affect the distribution and efficient use of scarce human and natural resources, serve as a tool for governments (particularly, as a means of affecting the outcome of military actions), permit the creation of new economic markets, and, ultimately, directly influence the quality of life for the individual. The second motor of history is the *individual's struggle for recognition.* This innate drive for significance and meaning in the presence of a much larger and potentially dehumanizing society causes individuals to fight for human dignity, to rise above their current conditions, and in the process, change themselves and often change the nature of the social institutions around them.

Fukuyama observes that these two forces tend to drive even culturally disparate societies toward capitalist democracies.[8] Consider, for example, the rate at which free international markets and representative governments

---

[7] Fukuyama, F. (1991). *The End of History and the Last Man.* New York, New York: The Free Press.

have been adopted during the past few decades. Today, democratic government is the dominant social structure, whereas in the 1700s, such structures were largely experimental. Fukuyama speaks of this as marking the end of history, because it represents a logical, stable, and final social organization.[9] Fukuyama goes on to observe that such an "end of history" engenders a crisis in the spiritual condition of man, manifest in the homogenization of society. The role of the so-called "last man" in this age is strikingly different than in previous ages.

As we study the growth and maturation of the computer sciences over the past half-century, we find markedly similar circumstances.

We suggest that there are two motors that drive advancements in software development. The first of these is the *logic and direction of modern software engineering*. Although we hesitate branding our development entirely as a science (compared to physics, for example), there has indeed been a clear, observable, and directed advancement in the industry's approach to the theories underlying software development. Second, *software development represents a struggle against complexity*. In the words of Fred Brook, complexity is an essential, not an accidental, property of all software.

Our premise is that these forces drive us toward object-oriented technology. To paraphrase Fukuyama, we speak of this as "the end of objects," meaning not that the object-oriented paradigm is already passé, but rather, that this paradigm denotes a logical, stable, and final organizing principle for software development. As a consequence, this leads us to consider the role of the individual developer (the so-called "last programmer") in the presence of this stable state.

Perhaps the most significant trend in software engineering has been the drive toward more expressive forms of abstraction. Starting with a focus

---

[8] Capitalist, in the sense of supporting free-market economies; democratic, in the sense of establishing a participatory form of government.

[9] As Larry Constantine has pointed out to me, we must always be wary of such sweeping conclusions. Every age has generally viewed itself as the pinnacle of human achievement, which no future generation could ever surpass. The same lesson undoubtedly applies to object-oriented technology and software engineering in general.

upon algorithmic abstraction in the 1950s and '60s, the '70s brought about a greater focus upon data abstraction and now, fueled to a large measure by work in abstract data types in the '70s and '80s, there is a focus upon object-oriented abstractions. (Actually, it goes back much further in history than this. Aristotle is perhaps the first person to have articulated the dichotomy of process- versus object-oriented abstraction.)

As Tokoro points out, "the term 'object' emerged almost independently in various fields in computer science, almost simultaneously in the early 1970s, to refer to notions that were different in their appearance, yet mutually related. All of these notions were invented to manage the complexity of software systems in such a way that objects represented components of a modularly decomposed system or modular units of knowledge representation."[10] Levy adds that the following events have contributed to the evolution of object-oriented concepts:

- Advances in computer architecture, including capability systems and hardware support for operating systems concepts

- Advances in programming languages, as demonstrated in Simula, Smalltalk, CLU, and Ada

- Advances in programming methodology, including modularization and information hiding (Levy 1984, 13)

We would add to this list three more contributions to the foundation of the object model:

- Advances in database models

- Research in artificial intelligence

- Advances in philosophy and cognitive science

---

[10] Yonezawa, A., & Tokoro, M. (1987). Object-oriented concurrent programming: An introduction. in *Object-Oriented Concurrent Programming*. Cambridge, MA: MIT Press, 1987. p. 2.

These lists suggest a remarkable confluence of ideas in very disparate elements of the computer sciences, all pointing toward object-oriented abstractions.

With regard to the struggle against complexity, Dr. Tim Standish has pointed out to me that one can never eliminate the complexity inherent in a software system, one can only hope to manage that complexity. We have elsewhere suggested that all well-structured systems that exhibit such organized complexity share five common characteristics (Booch 1991):

- Complexity takes the form of a hierarchy.

- The choice of what components in a system are primitive is relatively arbitrary and is largely up to the discretion of the observer.

- Intra-component linkages are generally stronger than inter-component linkages.

- Hierarchical systems are usually composed of only a few different kinds of subsystems in various combinations and arrangements.

- A complex system that works is invariably found to have evolved from a simple system that worked.

In all fairness, it is important to point out that there are local disturbances to this otherwise pristine picture of the object-oriented world. Business and economic factors introduce noise to this picture, manifest in a number of technology battlegrounds for which sometimes the biggest or first, not necessarily the technically superior, controls the outcome. For example, we have seen such conflict in the domain of operating systems (DOS versus Windows/NT versus Unix versus OS/2—the list goes on and on). Interestingly, however, the most recent generation of such operating systems at least presents an object-oriented model to the user and some, such as Microsoft's Windows/NT, have a much deeper object-oriented infrastructure. A related battle is playing itself out in the domain of graphical user interfaces (Motif versus Openlook versus Windows versus the Macintosh look and feel—and again the list continues). Continuing, there are fierce language wars ongoing (C versus C++ versus Smalltalk versus Ada versus COBOL) but again, the clear trend in modern programming languages has been the drive for support of the object-oriented paradigm. (Consider in particular the evolution of C++ from C, the adoption of object-oriented constructs by Ada in Ada95, and the object-oriented extensions to COBOL.)

Partly fueling these rather localized skirmishes are two fundamental technology trends, including:

- The drive toward greater distribution and connectivity, together with vastly increased bandwidth of networks

- The dramatic decline of the cost of MIPS and memory, culminating in surplus computing resources at the hands of the individual

Fueled by social and economic pressures that drive us to automate more and more domains, this drive toward object-oriented abstractions has lead to the application of the object-oriented paradigm to virtually every computational domain. At one extreme, we have encountered systems of global significance, such as for multinational banking, or Singapore's effort to computerize many aspects of its people's daily life. Here, the object-oriented paradigm is viewed as perhaps the *only* means of economically architecting an enduring system. At the other end of the spectrum, we have encountered the use of the object-oriented paradigm for such singular domains as pacemakers, bowling alley automation, cookie production, and public utility management.

In a manner of speaking, this indeed represents the end of objects: Object-orientation, in the steady state, is a stabilizing principle upon which we can organize the broadest spectrum of complex software systems.[11] Still, we observe that even in this steady state, software development will continue to involve a sea of strategic and tactical details. Ultimately, the speed and accuracy with which we can develop becomes a fundamental limiting factor in our ability to produce software.

---

[11] We completely acknowledge that not all domains are well-suited to the object-oriented paradigm, just as a liberal democracy is not well-suited to, for example, a nation emerging from a massive and overwhelming natural disaster. However, our discipline is sufficiently immature, such that we do not yet have sufficient information to predict what domains are most applicable, and what are not.

The element of the object-oriented paradigm which makes this such a stabilizing principle is that of architecture, or conceptual integrity, in Fred Brook's terms.

Consider architecture as viewed by architects of physical structures. This discipline distinguishes architecture from accidental organization by its:

- Suitability for use by human beings in general and its adaptability to particular human activities

- Stability and permanence of its construction

- Communication of experience and ideas through form

Structures such as cathedrals are typical of this model. The craft of designing cathedrals perhaps reached its pinnacle in the Middle Ages. Cathedrals such as the York Minster represented public facilities intended to last for centuries, and required a clear architectural vision, since the structure would likely not be completed in the lifetime of its original architect.

Now, software systems are not yet so long-lived, but the fluidity of our industry demands a similar focused architectural vision. Indeed, of the hundreds of object-oriented software developments we have encountered (many successful, several unsuccessful), the singular characteristic present in all the successful projects—and missing in the unsuccessful ones—was that of an architectural vision.

We define architectural vision as the crafting of systems that are constructed in well-defined layers of abstraction, for which there is a clear separation of concerns between the interface and the implementation of each layer; ultimately, we seek to build simple architectures, in which common behaviors are achieved through common mechanisms. We cannot state this point strongly enough: at all times, it is essential to maintain a clear vision of the system's strategic and tactical architecture.

Back to physical architectures, we may classify different structures by their form and function. Thus, we speak of domestic, religious, governmental, recreational, educational, and commercial architectures. Each genre of structure is so denoted by a unique set of properties, and so it is with object-oriented software systems.

Among the well-structured systems we have encountered, we have observed the following kinds of software architectures:

- Client/server
- GUI-centric
- DBMS-centric
- Intermediate representation-centric
- Blackboard
- Subsumption[12]

These all represent strategic architectures, meaning that they have a sweeping, global impact upon the overall origination of a system. On a more local level, we have the tactical architecture, which affects the patterns whereby objects collaborate with one another.

Return again to the domain of physical architectures. At the time of Michaelangelo, the study of machines led to the codification of certain kinds of simple machines, that—when assembled in ways unique to the given problem—provided some essential behavior. This classification included about 25 different kinds of machines such as screws, levers, gears, couplings, and belts.

Restating this in software terms, we call such simple machines *mechanisms*. Simply stated, a mechanism provides some system behavior through the behavior associated with a set of objects. In all nontrivial systems, we find such patterns of collaborating objects. In well-structured object-oriented systems, we usually find a small set of well-engineered mechanisms, which are reused again and again throughout the system. Because such abstractions are pervasive, it is for this reason that we state that the class is a

---

[12] Most of these kinds of architectures are likely intuitive, except for the last category. The concept of *subsumption* architectures has been pioneered by Dr. Rodney Brooks, of the MIT Artificial Intelligence Laboratory. Dr. Brook's work focuses on the creation of small, autonomous, insect-like robots. In subsumption architectures, there is no central locus of control; rather, each subsystem independently is responsible for a small set of behaviors and, like Minsky's concept of the society of mind, work together to form a whole whose behavior is much greater than that of the individual parts.

necessary, but insufficient, unit of decomposition. In other words, all non-trivial applications demand the presence of abstractions that cannot properly be captured in a single class.[13]

Just as for strategic architectures, we have observed a number of different kinds of mechanisms in well-structured object-oriented systems, including:
- Dependency
- Event handling
- Error detection
- Memory management
- Drawing
- Messaging
- Persistence

Ergo, we are arguing that, at the end of objects, the object-oriented paradigm continues to scale up: both strategic and tactical architectures are amenable to the object-oriented paradigm.

Why then do we say that, even at the end of objects, software development involves a sea of details? The root of this problem lies with the central problem of all things object-oriented: the discovery and invention of objects. How do we figure out what objects and classes to use in our system?

Classification is at the heart of this problem, for classification is the means whereby we order knowledge. Recognizing the sameness among things allows us to expose the commonalty within key abstractions and mechanisms. Unfortunately, our problem is made difficult, because there is no such thing as a "perfect" classification: There are profound classifications, and there are profoundly stupid ones. The role of the architect requires an ability to distinguish between the two.

The fact that classification is central to all things object oriented is what requires object-oriented software development to be both iterative and incremental. (Actually, the problem of classification is central to every scientific

---

[13] For example, the MVC paradigm in Smalltalk is not defined by any single class, but requires knowledge of this triad of classes; in C++, a single class is insufficient to express the abstraction of an entire GUI, such as Motif; rather, such a facility is best expressed as a set of collaborating classes.

discipline.) We speak of development as being iterative because it requires several cycles throughout the analysis/design/implement process; it is incremental because, at each cycle, we seek to reach closure a little bit at a time.

Of course, left to their own devices, programmers often never reach closure (...wherein Boehm's spiral model of software development becomes a *death spiral*). As Humphry has observed, the degree of discipline that exists in a software development organization is a measure of its maturity. He has proposed the following levels of process maturity:

- Chaotic
- Repeatable
- Defined
- Managed
- Optimizing

At the level of chaos, the development team is in freefall, meaning that the iterative and incremental process is out of control. In well-structured object-oriented systems, we have observed that there exists a balance between the unrestrained efforts of individual developers (which we speak of as the micro process of development) and a broader, disciplined effort by the team as a whole (which we speak of as the macro process). Stated another way, the micro process is closely related to Boehm's spiral model, and serves as the framework for an iterative and incremental approach to development; the micro model is what the individual developer does on a day-to-day basis. The macro process is more closely related to the traditional waterfall life-cycle, and serves as the controlling framework of the micro process; the macro model involves the successive refinement of architectural prototypes, each of which moves closer to the ultimately desired functionality of the end system.

This leads us to now consider the role of the individual developer, the so-called "last programmer." To this end, we distinguish among opposing roles.

First, we have the hacker versus the team player. The image of the hacker as the lone, Rambo-style programmer is appealing, perhaps because—given the fluidity of software—anything is possible... it's just a simple matter of programming. Indeed, some killer applications have emerged from lone developers (consider Visicalc, the forerunner to a whole industry of personal productivity tools such as Lotus 1-2-3, and which in turn helped fuel the dramatic growth in sales of personal computers). The problem with relying upon the individual super-developer is that economics dictate that most of the world's software development be achieved by mere mortals and we as an industry cannot really upon the (unpredictable) breakthroughs of individuals. (Although, in our industry, we seem to be able to create whole new markets overnight through the efforts of such individuals.) For this reason, we must consider, in the steady state, the last programmer as a team player.

Similarly, we have the analyst versus the designer versus the coder. In some organizations, these roles are strongly institutionalized—to the degree that some organizations build separate buildings for each group of people! Given the incremental and iterative nature of object-oriented software development, we prefer to consider a subtly different structure: the abstractionist versus the implementor.

Our experience has been that, in most object-oriented developments, some (but not all) of the developers have sound skills in finding and articulating abstractions, whereas others are better suited to taking such abstractions and assembling them to form some meaningful application. In the healthiest projects, there is a mutual respect between both kinds of developers, and a reasonable and manageable tension between the generality and pragmatics that each group, respectively, focuses upon. A project staffed with no abstractionists will generally never settle upon a resilient architecture, and similarly, a project staffed with only abstractionists will tend to over-engineer the architecture, and devise unimplementable mechanisms.

CONDUCTING A SOFTWARE ARCHITECTURE ASSESSMENT

I spend about 30 to 40% of my time as an architectural mentor. (This is in keeping with my philosophy that you shouldn't trust a methodologist who doesn't use his or her own method.) Practically, this means that organizations bring me in to assess the health of their project and of their architecture, and to offer advice on what they should do to move forward. My engagements are split fairly evenly between organizations just starting a project and organizations whose projects are at some key decision point. The latter typically involves projects between release cycles as well as projects in crisis. It is from these projects that you may have heard a few of my horror stories:

> *This particular project in crisis had written several hundred thousands of lines of C++. A quick review revealed that the team had written lots of code, but not one single class.*

> *Another project was similarly in crisis. A quick review here revealed that the team had written hundreds of thousands of lines of C++, and that they had about the expected number of classes for that size system. However, further investigation revealed that, on the average, each class had about one member function, usually named with some variation of the verb "do it."*

The vast majority of the projects that I encounter are all trying to do the *Right Thing*, but simply need another set of experienced eyes to put them or to keep them on the right path.

This is in fact the purpose of a software architecture assessment: *to assess the health of a project as viewed from its architecture, its organization, and its process.* Any project of scale can benefit from having periodic assessments, which serve at least three goals:

- Assessments force risks to the success of the project to become visible, making it possible to devise a plan for mitigating those risks

- Assessments give the project an opportunity to make mid-course corrections

- Assessments give the team a sense of closure, by acknowledging what has been accomplished

You don't have to bring in a hired hand to do an assessment. The practices I'll tell you about here can be conducted internally. (Although it's often said that "an expert is somebody from out of town." Having an external assessor is particularly useful for exposing areas of risk for which the project is in denial.)

Politically charged projects often resist such assessments because they do in fact force risks to the surface, and that is sometimes viewed as threatening to the project's management. In such cases, a software architecture assessment is exactly what's needed, because the fact that the team is trying to ignore its risks is in itself a warning sign of imminent failure. Many times, the risks identified during an assessment come as no surprise to a few of the project's developers, but they sometimes blind-side the project's management. Similarly, many assessments turn out to be an eye-opening experience for the developers, because only by looking at the project from a 35,000-foot view do they begin to understand all the outside forces that shape their management's decisions (which, from the trenches, may look arbitrary and capricious).

The very process of conducting a software architecture assessment has value, because it forces the team to communicate among its members and to organize its thoughts about the project's architecture. I find that if, in preparation for an assessment, a project ceases normal activities and spends days getting ready, this itself is a warning sign there's something fundamentally wrong. Healthy projects require minimal preparation, simply because they have already internalized the importance of architecture and have organized their team and their process accordingly.

A colleague of mine, Philippe Kruchten describes the process of conducting an architectural assessment in the following algorithm:[14]

```
Define the exact question(s) or focus: what assessment, why?
Define the team, the agenda, the necessary information
Obtain the information
    Technical briefings
    "Mine" the architecture/define scenarios/measure
loop
    Interview/examine/read/compare
```

---

[14] Among his other duties, Philippe has served as the architect of the Canadian Air Traffic Control System.

```
      Identify potential issues
      Confirm they are issues
      Identify improvement or change
  end loop
  Prepare draft report and recommendations
  Review draft report, eliminate bias, refine actions
  Prepare final report
  Present conclusions
  Exploit the results/follow up on actions
```

The essence of this process is to nail down the issues to be examined, explore the architecture, the organization, and the processes, and then act on those issues.

Depending upon the size of the project, a typical assessment might take anywhere from a day to a couple of weeks. In my engagements, on the average, I'll spend about two days every quarter for large projects, meaning those with a staff of a few dozen developers building several hundred thousand to a million lines of code. The value of scheduling these reviews on a periodic basis is that this allows you to see long-term trends, yet still allowing time for the project to institute mid-course corrections.

I could write a whole book on the details of conducting a software architecture assessment, but let me at least offer here some of the A-level issues that I tend to cover. I must admit that it is hard to generalize, and therefore I can't present a cookbook of what to do. Every project is different, and those differences lead you to different areas to attack. I'll cover the project's architecture, its organization, and its process.

ARCHITECTURE

With regard to the architecture, the first question to ask is simply, *"Is there a defined architecture?"* If the answer is no, then this is indeed a project in need of serious help. The proper response is either to (a) craft an architecture and develop a plan for incrementally imposing it upon the system, or (b) flee. Sometimes a project is just beyond help, and usually the humane thing in such a case is to put it out of its misery.

If there is a defined architecture, then the next series of questions begin to address the nature of that architecture. First, does the whole team see the architecture the same way? Interviewing team members one-on-one, away from their management, is a great way to discover if the project's policies are in fact being put into practice. Asking simple yet fundamental questions like "what is the meaning of a customer class?" to developers at different levels of the system is very telling, because consistency is an indication of a strong architectural presence, and inconsistency is an indication of architectural rot.

Although there are many ways to show a software architecture, the Booch Method encourages the use of a class diagram of categories, showing the logical separation of concerns. Figure 1 is a simple example in the UML, showing packages and their dependencies:

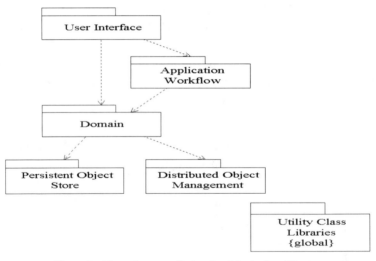

Figure 1. Class diagram of a top-level logical architecture.

Second, I check to see: *Does the project solves common problems in common ways*? For example, what's the mechanism for exception handling? What about storage management? Is there a standard look-and-feel in the GUI, and a standard way of accessing persistent data? Basically, these questions are a search for two things: A search for the use of patterns, and a search for the project's approach to problems that crop up in every system of scale.

In studying a project's architecture, I'll also look at a few key metrics, for example:

- The number of classes vis-à-vis the number of lines of code

- The distribution of responsibilities among classes

- The number of categories in the system and the number of classes/ mechanisms per category

Experience shows that there's a balance to look for here. For example, a system with just 10 classes and 100,000 lines of code is probably out of whack. Similarly, a system with 1,000 classes and only a couple of categories is probably similarly out of whack.

ORGANIZATION

When assessing a project's *team* itself, I'll address the following issues:

- Is there an identifiable architect?

- What's the relationship between the project's management and its developers?

- What's the relationship between the project and its patron?

- Are end users a part of the scene at all?

- For larger projects, is there an identifiable middle layer of technical management?

Basically, these questions are a search for one thing: Is the team organized to encourage multiple paths of communication, or is this an ossified group that relies upon high ceremony to carry out its business?

PROCESS

When assessing the team's *process*, there's one big question that I address first:

- Does the project have a *regular rhythm of releases?*

In other words, has an incremental and iterative process been instituted? Projects in crisis tend to run at a frantic pace, generating new releases opportunistically. Projects in stasis tend to have no regular releases, but instead push back all their risk to one big-bang integration event. What I look for here is a regular release schedule (for example, weekly for internal releases, every few months for external releases). If answers to this question reveal that the project has no rhythm, the proper reaction is to exert some control over the project to make it start beating at a regular pace.

Other process questions that I'll address include:

- What reviews are conducted?

- What metrics are collected?

- What tangible artifacts are being created, other than just the software itself?

The presence or absence of reviews, metrics, and artifacts is very telling. Projects in crisis will tend to abandon all three while in the heat of battle, never to find the time to return to them. Healthy projects, on the other hand, will tend to conduct architecture reviews as well as more frequent peer reviews. Similarly, unhealthy projects will tend to ignore formal metrics, while healthy ones will at least follow basics such as defect density, defect discovery, and architectural churn.[15] Finally, the absence of any meaningful documentation is the sign of a project on the edge of meltdown; the presence of the right documents (e.g., an architectural description) is a very good sign.

DELIVERING THE ASSESSMENT

At the end of an assessment, it's wrong to publish a report and then ride away into the sunset. Rather, the most effective software architecture assessment must do three things:

- *Provide a frank assessment on the state of the project.* To do otherwise is to deny reality.

- *Identify areas of risk.* In other words, what issues will prevent the project from meeting its measure of success?

---

[15] *Architectural churn* is a measure of the rate of change of a system. Tracking what parts of the system are changing most rapidly is a good predictor of where there are architectural problems.

- *Establish a plan of action to mitigate those risks.*

Sometimes, reporting on assessment requires great tact and diplomacy. Projects need to hear the good news, as well as the bad, and that sometimes means saying things that upset the political structure of the organization. However, if the team's focus is upon building quality software and not building empires, then no matter how distasteful the message, a frank assessment will only serve to make the project healthier.

DISTRIBUTED SYSTEMS

Simply put, a distributed system is one whose GUI, data, and/or computational elements are in some manner physically distributed. Ultimately, almost every real system is amenable to some degree of distribution. Distributed systems are thus in their own right worthy of study, because they introduce a level of complexity all of their own. There is a vast chasm between building an isolated, single-user application for a dedicated personal computer versus building a globally distributed system consisting of dozens of different collaborating programs running on multiple computers.

The study of distributed systems is important for another very practical reason, namely, that in more and more domains, requirements dictate that resources be physically distributed. That demand, coupled with the sinking costs of high-bandwidth networking, means that distributed systems are becoming pervasive.

Joe Firmage from Novell makes this same observation in a very concise way.[16] He suggests that applications can be grouped into one of five categories, according to their degree of distribution:

> *Network-ignorant* — The application is essentially isolated, other than perhaps sharing distant resources made to appear local through redirection by the underlying operating system.

---

[16] Firmage, J. (1995). Five software models. *Byte*, May 1995, p. 50.

Network-aware — The application is deliberately distributed across a network, and the application itself has some sense of its physical distribution, which is typically rigidly defined.

True partitioning — The application consists of a number of relatively independent yet collaborating peer components that are physically distributed, and perhaps may even migrate.

Terminal/host — This is a classical client/server decomposition, consisting of a heavy server and lighter weight clients that do some local computation that off-load the server.

Traditional mainframe — just as it sounds: the application basically resides on a large server, accessed by relatively dumb clients that do little, if any, computation.

Firmage goes on to predict that the future of computation lies in the third category, *true partitioning*. If that's true—and I happen to agree with him—then life will only get more interesting for every application development team that must cope with the additional complexity inherent in such architectures.

This is where methods are relevant. It is clear that object-oriented methods are already good at modeling a large class of systems, and so it is desirable to apply them to the modeling of these emerging distributed systems.

The Booch Method already addresses some issues associated with modeling distributed systems. In fact, it is one of the few notations that has any semantics dealing with physical distribution. As illustrated in Figure 2, Deployment Diagrams exist in the UML notation so developers can specify and visualize the physical topology of a system. (A Deployment diagrams is the UML successor to the Booch Process diagram.) The semantics of this notation include a mapping from processors to processes, and a mapping from processes to classes and objects. These semantics help, but unfortunately few object-oriented tools currently exploit this aspect of the notation.

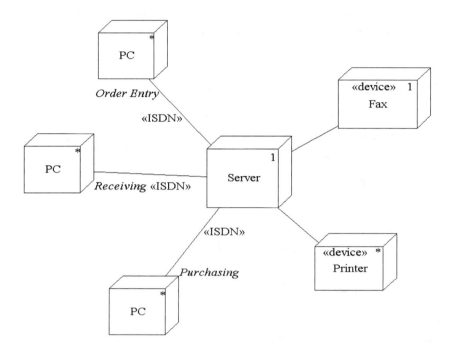

Figure 2. A deployment diagram.

Having now worked with a number of distributed systems, I've begun to realize that these semantics are necessary but insufficient. Believe me, adding notation is something I've very reluctant to do, but here, some tightening of current semantics and a little creative reuse of existing notation seems to be in order, especially if you understand my goals. Specifically, I want a notation that is expressive enough so that developers can specify and visualize all the important decisions regarding a system's distribution, and that is complete enough so that a large degree of code generation and reverse engineering is possible. I should state that one of the reasons I'm optimistic that this is not only desirable but also possible, is the growing identification of common patterns of distribution that can readily be codified in object-oriented terms.[17]

To address these dual goals of visualization and construction, it is important to first understand what issues are germane to distributed systems. In my experience, all the other usual issues of modeling complex systems apply, but there are five additional topics that must be considered when building a distributed one, namely:

Distribution — the physical allocation of classes and objects (including processes) to processors in the network.

Clustering — the physical grouping of classes and objects guaranteed to co-exist on the same processor.

Synchronization — the synchronization of message passing among distributed objects.

Interfaces — the physical separation of interfaces (which define services) from implementations (which provide services).

Migration — the movement of classes and objects (including processes) in the network.

I'll address each of these issues in turn, although realize that they interact in subtle ways, as I'll point out.

DISTRIBUTION

In the simplest sense, a distributed object-oriented system is one whose classes and objects are all logically part of a single domain model, yet physically may be spread across a network of machines. This implies, therefore, an equivalent distribution of processes that animate these objects. In more complex systems, distribution may involve the migration of objects and processes from one machine to another over time.

From this perspective, it's important to understand what can be meaningfully distributed in a system. First, classes can be distributed. In practice, this

---

[17] There is more depth to this statement that I can begin to explain here. Suffice it to say that, at the summer 1995 PLoP (a workshop on Pattern Languages of Programs, hosted by the Hillside group), a large number of the patterns presented and discussed dealt with distribution. This is an encouraging sign, because it means that a number of people are addressing the same issues, and more important, are discovering common solutions to these common problems.

means taking a system's domain model and then allocating parts of them to different processors. For example, in a transportation system, one might have a number of classes directly associated with shipments, whose realizations physically reside on a machine at a trucking depot. Clearly, with this kind of allocation, objects of such classes can only reside on the machine or machines where those classes are also defined. Second, objects can be distributed. If the class for a shipment physically lives on machines at different trucking depots, then it is possible to have different shipment objects reside on different machines.

By implication, processes and programs can be distributed. In the Booch notation, processes and threads are identified as active objects, and so it follows that processes and threads can be distributed in the same manner as simple objects. The same is true for programs. If we reify the concept of a program (meaning that we treat a program as an object), then it too can be seen as distributed.

None of what I've said so far goes beyond the existing Booch notation, except to clarify a few semantics. Specifically, as suggested in Figure 2, the following semantics apply:

- On a deployment diagram, one may attach the name of a class or an object to a node/processor.

- The same class may appear on multiple nodes/processors.

- At any one point in time, the same object may appear on exactly one node/processor.

- By implication, a class may denote a family of processes, threads, or programs.

- By implication, an object may denote a specific process, thread, or program.

In the presence of a tool that captures these semantics, then it is clear that navigation in either direction is possible, namely, from a class (in a class diagram), an object (in an collaboration diagram), or a program (in a deployment diagram) to a processor as well as from a processor to a class, object, or module.

There are two additional notational issues that we have addressed:

- Classes and objects icons may be adorned with a property value (and optional tag) which specifies their location, for example: *location=server.*

- Processes, threads, and programs can be distinguished by the use of a stereotype adornment on a class or object, for example, *«process»*.

CLUSTERING

Distributing individual classes and objects is important, but it's not very realistic. In practice, groups of classes and objects tend to be distributed together. In fact, knowing that certain classes and objects always reside on the same processor is a wonderfully simplifying assumption, because it means that each can send messages to one another locally. Furthermore, this assumption can be preserved even if they as a group migrate to another processor. Among different groups, these semantics mean that cross-group messaging may be local (if the groups happen to reside on the same processor) or it may be remote (if the groups happen to reside on different processors).

This observation leads to a new concept, which I'll call a *distribution unit.*[18] A distribution unit has these semantics:

- A *distribution unit* is a named grouping of classes and/or objects, which includes the name of a processor upon which the group resides.

- The membership of a distribution unit may vary.

- The location of a distribution unit may vary.

- The members of a single distribution unit are therefore guaranteed to communicate locally; the members of different distribution units may

---

[18] This idea is not of my invention. Rather, it comes from some colleague at a European telephony company, whom I unfortunately cannot reveal at the moment for reasons of nondisclosure.

communicate locally (if their units happen to coexist on the same processor) or remotely (if their units don't coexist).

Combining these semantics with the central semantics of distribution
described in the previous section yields the following:

- By implication, on a deployment diagram, one may attach the name of
a distribution unit to a node/processor.

Figure 3 provides an example of a class diagram that I've partitioned.
Here, I've applied a creative use of notation.

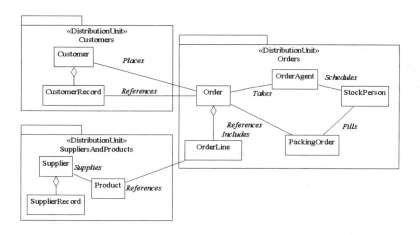

Figure 3. Class diagram with distribution units.

This is just a representative example: I've not illustrated a tremendously
profound or even optimal partitioning, but rather just want to offer a representative example. Furthermore, on this diagram, I've not indicated the location of any of the distribution units (that is, its location in the network).

SYNCHRONIZATION

Once you begin to distribute objects, then all sorts of other design issues pop
up. How do objects send messages across processors? How does one object
even find another to send a message to it? Indeed, it is exactly this kind of
partitioning that has yielded a very powerful middleware abstraction, that of

an Object Request Broker (ORB). ORBs are sort of the plumbing of a distributed system, and ultimately have responsibility for two basic behaviors:

> *Object registration* — The problem of unique object identity across address spaces
>
> *Object messaging* — The problem of sending messages to a distant object

Using ORBs as a basic architectural building block leads to a model of distribution that is really quite straightforward. For example, consider one object sending a message to another object. From the outside, this looks like a typical method dispatch from one object to another. Under the sheets in the middleware, this turns into a request to an ORB, who locates the object in the network, given its unique identity. If the object is indeed local, then the message passing proceeds as usual. If the object is remote, the ORB establishes a proxy, packs the message for transmission across the network, ensures its delivery, unpacks the message at the side of the remote object, and then completes the connection.

A common approach to the implementation of ORBs is the use of remote procedure calls (RPCs), which represent a fairly stable and proven technology. The value of an ORB is to hide the details of such a mechanism, and add the behaviors associated with object registration and distribution.

The semantics of an ORB can be represented in the Booch notation. In Figure 4, I've expressed the general semantics of a forwarding broker, which is the mechanism used by the OMG CORBA (Object Management Group Common Object Request Broker Architecture).[19] This diagram uses the basic notation for collaboration diagrams, supplemented with packages, which are used here to designate units of distribution.

---

[19] This figure is adapted from Figure 4a in Adler, R.(1995, April). Distributed coordination models for client/server computing. *IEEE Computer,* p. 17.

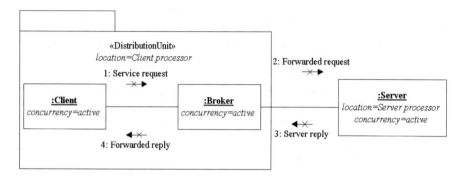

Figure 4. Collaboration diagram showing synchronization via a forwarding broker.

This diagram represents a vast simplification, because the broker does a lot more than this simple messaging implies. Indeed, because in this case we've modeled messaging across distribution units, the underlying mechanisms that connect the client and broker objects is fundamentally different than that between the broker and the server. This is where the remote procedure calls that connect the server and the broker come into play, but in a manner that is transparent to the client.

INTERFACES

Now that we have the semantics of basic distribution, plus clustering and synchronization, another element comes into play, namely, the publishing, registration, and implementation of *interfaces*. In the context of CORBA (and other mechanisms for middleware distribution), it is common to use an Interface Definition Language (IDL) to specify the interface of a class of objects. The use of an IDL introduces another level of implementation complexity, but it does allow a programming language-independent specification of a class. This means that the client of a class (which uses an interface) and the realization of that interface can actually be developed with widely varying technologies.

From the perspective of a typical client, the use of IDL can be pushed down to the point where it is largely invisible. However, if we take this concept of interface a little further, it's clear that it has some wider reaching implications. Specifically, when modeling a larger system, it is common to

159

define categories of classes. Some of these classes may be visible by clients outside this category, so in fact, these clients really only care about interfaces. Now, couple this with the fact that, in distributed systems, these categories of classes are also typically isomorphic to distribution units, and we begin to see interfaces that straddle processor boundaries.

To distinguish the specification and the realization of such interfaces, it is useful to mark an interface using an adornment as shown in Figure 5.

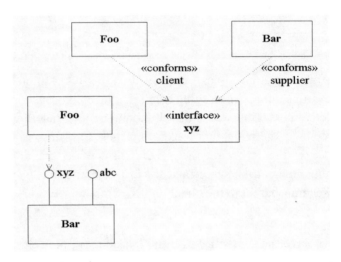

Figure 5. Class diagram showing reified and symbolic interface notation.

The semantics of these adornments are quite simple: An *interface* defines a protocol that clients can rely upon and implementations are obligated to satisfy.

Interface semantics may be applied to utilities as well. In fact, in the context of open systems, it's probably the case that utility interfaces are the more common occurrence, since their semantics, by implication, really define an API.

Interface semantics have a bearing not just for distributed systems, but are useful for other modeling problems as well. In particular, by explicitly distinguishing interfaces, it is possible to model type hierarchies versus class hierarchies (which are combined in most object-oriented programming languages). It is a common Smalltalk idiom, for example, to have classes of objects that conform to a common protocol. In essence, this means that the classes really represent the same type, even though they may not be united by a common inheritance lattice.

MIGRATION

In certain classes of systems, objects (and processes and programs) are not only distributed, but they migrate as well. For example, consider an object representing an aircraft in an air-traffic control system. Logically, there is exactly one such software object for every real aircraft in the context of this system. Physically, however, this object must migrate, for reasons of performance and locality of reference. If a real plane takes off from San Francisco and travels to Denver, then in the software system, we'd like the object representing this aircraft to migrate from nodes in California to nodes in Colorado. (We'd also like the real luggage to migrate as well, but that fantasy is, of course, beyond the scope of this article.)

The same kind of migration can occur among processes. For example, in certain mission-critical systems, if a processor goes down, then it is common to restart the moribund processes on a healthy processor. Logically, this implies a migration of processes.

To be honest, modeling the migration of objects pushes the limits of a purely static notation. In practice, migration is an activity that can be expressed in a collaboration diagram, although animation of a collaboration diagram in a tool is something that can yield far better visualization.

SUMMARY

Building distributed systems is really hard, and its problems are not going to go away. As I've shown, however, the judicious use of a notation can help greatly in visualizing the semantics of distribution. With the right tool support, and with the growing maturity of middleware for CORBA and other technologies, much of the implementation complexity can be hidden from developers, so that they can then focus on the broader system issues of distribution, namely, crafting a balanced distribution of resources and tuning it so that it yields reasonable performance.

PATTERNS

I'm generally not an excitable person. My idea of a great summer after-noon is reading a book alongside some crisp Colorado mountain stream, miles away from anything containing a transistor. Not quite the excitement of bungee jumping or, perhaps even more intense, subclassing from a deep class lattice while mixing in a couple of other abstract base classes to achieve some desired polymorphic behavior... Neither activity is for the faint of heart. However, there is one emerging development in the world of objects that does genuinely excite me, and that is the methodical identification of *patterns*.

First, let me introduce some of the key players. There are a number of cen-ters of gravity in this great search, one in the United States, and another in the United Kingdom. In the U.S., one such group includes the diverse talents of Ralph Johnson (University of Illinois), Erich Gamma, and John Vlissides (both from Taligent), and Richard Helm (IBM). Although not a part of this association, Mary Shaw, Rebecca Wirfs-Brock, and Peter Coad have inde-pendently contributed to the study of patterns. In the U.K., Bruce Anderson (University of Essex) has catalyzed significant study into the codification of patterns, and at OOPSLA '91 and '92 conferences, established workshops focused on the creation of an architecture handbook, whose purpose is ulti-mately to serve as a catalog of patterns.

The notion of patterns is significant, especially to all things object ori-ented, because it represents a higher leverage form of reuse. The search for patterns encompasses far more than finding the One Perfect Class, but rather, focuses upon identifying the common behavior and interactions that tran-scend individual objects.

The study of patterns is not unique to software. Indeed, the importance of patterns has long been recognized in other technical disciplines such as biology, chemistry, physics, and architecture. In a manner of speaking, the field of software engineering is just beginning to awaken to the importance of patterns. For example, Herbert Simon, in his study of complexity, observed that "hierarchic systems are usually composed of only a few different kinds of subsystems in various combinations and arrangements." In other words, *complex systems have common patterns*. These patterns may involve the reuse of small components, such as the cells found in both plants and animals, or of larger structures, such as vascular systems, also found in both plants and animals. In his classic work, *The Sciences of the Artificial,* Simon went on to illustrate how these patterns manifest themselves in social and biological systems, and how the existence of such patterns help to simplify their inherent complexity.

The oft-referenced Christopher Alexander has made similar observations to the domain of architecture, and his work has instigated a minor revolution in that field. He notes that, for the architect, "his act of design, whether humble, or gigantically complex, is governed entirely by the patterns he has in his mind at that moment, and his ability to combine these patterns to form a new design." Perhaps a bit dramatically, he goes on to suggest that "the more living patterns there are in a place—a room, a building, or a town—the more it comes to life as an entirety, the more it glows, the more it has that self-maintaining fire which is the *quality without a name.*"

I have found the same to be true in well-structured object-oriented systems. Using the terms suggested by Rob Murray, I distinguish between the strategic and tactical design decisions. A *strategic decision* is one that has sweeping architectural implications, such as the decision to use a particular client/server architecture, or the use of a certain OODBMS or GUI model. A *tactical decision* is one that has more local implications, such as the protocol of a specific class, or the signature of a member function. Both are important to the success of a software system, no matter what measure one gives to "success." Most important, perhaps, our strategic decisions have the greatest impact on our ability to craft simple, elegant architectures.

In object-oriented systems, strategic decisions manifest themselves in the form of class lattices (which capture our decisions about the static relationships among abstractions) and collaborations of objects (which capture our decisions about the common interactions among our abstractions). Several years ago, I suggested the term "*mechanism*" to describe any such structure whereby objects collaborate to provide some behavior that satisfies a requirement of the problem. Whereas the design of a class embodies the knowledge of how individual objects behave, a mechanism is a design decision about how collections of objects cooperate. Mechanisms thus represent patterns of behavior.

Whereas abstractions reflect the vocabulary of the problem domain, mechanisms are the soul of the design. During the design process, the developer must consider not only the design of individual classes, but also how instances of these classes work together. Lately, I have been influenced by the work of Kenny Rubin and Adele Goldberg (on object behavior analysis) and Ivar Jacobson (on use-case analysis), whose ideas suggest the use of scenarios to discover these collaborations. In a sense, the use of scenarios drives the whole analysis-and-design process. Once a developer decides upon a particular pattern of collaboration, the work is distributed among many objects by defining suitable methods in the appropriate classes. Ultimately, the protocol of an individual class encompasses all the operations required to implement all the behavior and all the mechanisms associated with each of its instances.

One of the contributions Linnaeus made to the field of botany was the suggestion that patterns may be found in the very patterns of animal and plant structure and behavior. I am no Linnaeus, but let me suggest a similar classification of patterns in object-oriented systems.

As it turns out, mechanisms are actually in the middle of a spectrum of patterns we find in well-structured software systems. At the low end of the food chain, we have idioms. An *idiom* is an expression peculiar to a certain programming language or application culture, representing a generally accepted convention for use of the language. Richard Gabriel, one of the architects of CLOS, has helped me understand that one defining characteristic of an idiom is that ignoring or violating the idiom has immediate social consequences: you are branded as a yahoo, or worse, an outsider. For example, in CLOS, no programmer would use underscores in function or variable names, although this is common practice in Ada. In C++, there are many such idioms inherited from the C culture, such as idioms for indexing and error handling. Part of the effort in learning a programming language is learning its idioms, which are usually passed down as folklore from programmer to programmer. However, as Jim Coplien has pointed out, idioms play an important role in codifying low-level patterns. He notes that "many common programming tasks [are] idiomatic" and therefore identifying such idioms allows "using C++ constructs to express functionality outside the language proper, while giving the illusion of being part of the language."

At the high end of the food chain, we have frameworks. A *framework* is a collection of classes that provide a set of services for a particular domain; a framework thus exports a number of individual classes and mechanisms that clients can use or adapt. Frameworks represent patterns and, hence, reuse "in the large."

Whereas idioms are part of a programming culture, frameworks are often the product of commercial ventures. For example, Apple's MacApp (and its successor, the Apple/Symantec Bedrock project) are both application frameworks written in C++ for building applications that conform to Macintosh user interface standards. Similarly, the Microsoft Foundation Class library (MFC) and Borland's ObjectWindows library (OWL) are frameworks for building applications that conform to the Windows user-interface standards. In each case, we find more than a bag of independent classes. Rather, the most mature architectures consist of a set of classes plus a modest number of well-articulated mechanisms that serve to animate these classes. In MacApp, for example, there are clear mechanisms for drawing in a window, for saving data in a document, and for cutting/copying/pasting across applications using the clipboard.

Most interesting patterns within frameworks are domain dependent. Recently, I have encountered commercial efforts to build frameworks in such diverse domains as patient health care, securities trading, and telephone switching systems. Across these domains, these products are architecturally very different. However, within each vertical application domain, there are clear patterns of idioms and mechanisms that serve to simplify the problem at hand.

In the domain of GUI-centric systems, for example, there are a number of such patterns: consider the mechanism for drawing things in a window. Several objects must collaborate to present an image to a user: a window, a view, the model being viewed, and some client that knows when (but not how) to display this model. The client first tells the window to draw itself. Since it may encompass several subviews, the window next tells each of its subviews to draw themselves. Each subview in turn tells its model to draw itself, ultimately resulting in an image shown to the user. In this mechanism, the model is entirely decoupled from the window and view in which it is presented: views can send messages to models, but models cannot send messages to views. Smalltalk uses a variation of this mechanism, and calls it the model-view-controller (MVC) architecture. A similar mechanism is employed in almost every object-oriented graphical user interface framework.

In Smalltalk, the MVC architecture in turn builds on another mechanism, the dependency mechanism, which is embodied in the behavior of the Smalltalk base class (whose name is the class Object), and thus pervades the entire Smalltalk class library.

Johnson and Anderson, together with their respective colleagues, have begun to enumerate and codify the patterns they have found in object-oriented systems. At the low end of the food chain, for example, we have patterns for double dispatching (faking the semantics of multiple polymorphism in a mono-polymorphic language such as C++ or Smalltalk), and delegation (a common pattern for distributing behavior within whole/part structures). In the middle of the food chain, the domain of mechanisms, we have patterns such as MVC, plus patterns for message passing, command interpretation, and error handling. At the high end of the food chain, we have patterns for whole applications, such as blackboard architectures (a central architecture for many systems embodying opportunistic control) and subsumption architectures (an architectural pattern suggested by Rodney Brooks at MIT, for structuring processes in autonomous robots).

Identifying patterns in software systems is hard, but ultimately pays off in the form of simpler, more resilient architectures. My observation is that this identification involves both discovery and invention. Through discovery, we come to recognize the key abstractions and mechanisms that form the vocabulary of our problem domain. Through invention, we devise generalized abstractions as well as new mechanisms that specify how objects collaborate. Ultimately, discovery and invention are both problems of classification, and classification is fundamentally a problem of finding sameness. When we classify, we seek to group things that have a common structure or exhibit a common behavior.

Crafting object-oriented systems is thus far more than what the naive object-oriented zealot will tell you, namely, to focus on inheritance lattices: inheritance is important, but it is not the only important thing. Rather, for all the kinds of patterns we have described here, patterns of behavior represent an intelligent distribution of responsibilities among a collection of classes; inheritance allows us to express these patterns with elegance and simplicity, but the very distribution of behavior is what is central to the meaning of each pattern. It is therefore the task of the developer to distribute such behaviors so that they may be combined in interesting ways, giving rise to the "self-maintaining fire" that is the mark of a profound object-oriented architecture.

PATTERNS & PROTOCOLS

Much has been written of late about the patterns movement. In my professional opinion, patterns are, well, *very cool.*

If you have been exposed to the concept of patterns in object-oriented systems, you are probably already familiar with the Gang of Four and their classic work, *Design Patterns* (Gamma et al. 1995). Their book makes two novel contributions to the field. First, *Design Patterns* introduces the concept of patterns as an essential element of crafting architectures for complex systems. Imposing meaningful patterns upon a system's architecture can not only improve its conceptual integrity, but in the best case can also make that system simpler. Second, their work identifies almost two dozen concrete patterns that can be used to build systems. This means that we now have a common vocabulary by which to name common solutions to common problems.

Another source of information about patterns comes from the Hillside Group, a nonprofit organization of sixteen individuals focused upon the science and the practice of patterns. The Hillside Group organizes an annual workshop on patterns called *Pattern Languages of Programs* (*PLoP*) and additionally has orchestrated a patterns mailing list.[20] One of the Hillside Group's founding members, Ralph Johnson, manages a patterns web page.[21] A number of other individuals have also made important contributions to this field, most notably Peter Coad and Wolfgang Pree. More recently, Mary Shaw and David Garland have written a book on software architecture that begins to address the issue of large architectural patterns (Shaw & Garland 1996).

Beyond the rhetoric, the important thing about patterns is that they really do add value. In just the past month, I've worked with a number of projects that actively use the Gamma patterns to shape their systems. During architecture reviews, I'll encounter developers from these projects who make mention of the Gamma patterns to describe their work. In the most productive organizations, I find developers who not only use the Gamma patterns, but go on to create their own patterns specific to their domain.

One interesting characteristic about the most sophisticated patterns is that each represents both a thing as well as a process. A pattern is a thing in that it denotes a particular collaboration of classes and objects and its resulting behavior. A pattern is a process in the sense that it not only describes a structure, but also a means of generating an instance of that structure in the context of a real system.[22] Furthermore—and this is going to sound very Zen— the best patterns disappear once they manifest themselves in a system.

As I've explained elsewhere (Booch 1996), patterns can be classified as idioms, mechanisms, or frameworks. An *idiom* is an expression peculiar to a certain programming language or organizational culture, and represents a generally accepted convention in that context. Idioms are thus a pattern that represent reuse in the small. For example, a particular style of declaring exception classes, stated in a project's programming style guide, is an idiom. A *mechanism*, on the other hand, is a structure whereby objects collaborate

---

[20] *patterns@cs.uiuc.edu.*

[21] *http://st-www.cs.uiuc.edu/users/patterns/patterns.html.*

[22] These are known as *generative* patterns.

to provide some behavior that satisfies a requirement of the problem domain. A mechanism is thus a design decision about how certain collections of objects cooperate. Mechanisms are the soul of a system's architecture, because their consistent use gives a conceptual integrity that solves common problems in common ways. All of the Gamma patterns are in fact mechanisms. Finally, a *framework* is a microarchitecture, denoting a collection of classes and mechanisms that together provide a set of services for a particular domain, which clients can use as well as adapt. We distinguish a framework from a simple class library by the fact that frameworks generally have control mechanisms such that the framework calls client operations. In a class library, it's usually the reverse: clients mainly invoke operations from the library. Thus, a framework is a kind of pattern that provides reuse in the large. Most of Shaw's patterns represent frameworks.

Notice what I've done thus far: I've described patterns as important architectural elements, as critical to developing object-oriented systems as much as are classes and objects. However—and here's the problem—no mainstream object-oriented method has yet treated a pattern as a thing that can and should be modeled.

In working on the Unified Modeling Language, Jim, Ivar, and I have begun to explore the notion of reifying patterns. In the remainder of this article, let me present our current thinking. I must emphasize that we have not completely worked out the semantics of this proposal, nor have we necessarily committed to making this an official part of UML.

Before I offer a solution, let me make clear the problem we are trying to solve:

> In modeling an object-oriented system, how can I represent the use of a pattern?

In other words, since patterns are a part of a developer's vocabulary, how can we make patterns a first-class citizen of the modeling language the developer uses to build systems? This question raises a number of secondary questions:

- How can I specify a mechanism?

- How can I show conformance to a mechanism?

- How does this relate to the semantics of protocols and contracts?

- What does this mean for specifying the semantics of frameworks?

I've left idioms out of the discussion, simply because they are largely at the level of the programming language, and hence are best described outside of UML.

The specification of mechanisms is something that the patterns community has been experimenting with for some time now. The classic Alexanderian approach is to specify a pattern as a "solution to a problem in a context."[23] Gamma and his colleagues expand upon this theme, and specify each of their patterns by stating its:

- Name/Kind
- Intent
- Motivation
- Applicability
- Structure
- Participants
- Collaborations
- Consequences
- Implementation
- Sample Code
- Known Uses
- Related Patterns

Much of this specification is done in text, together with a few well-placed class and object diagrams.

For example, consider one common Gamma pattern, chain of responsibility (Gamma et al. 1995, 223). This is a pattern often found in event-driven systems (especially GUI systems). The basic idea of this pattern is that a client sends a message to a handler, asking it to handle some request. That

---

[23] This term refers to Christopher Alexander, author of *The Timeless Way of Building* (1979) and *A Pattern Language* (1977). These two books have shaped a lot of the thinking in the patterns movement.

handler is actually part of a chain of handlers, and so either handles the request directly, or passes on the request to its successor. This delegation continues until the request floats up to a handler that takes responsibility for the request.

Gamma shows the structure of this pattern in a class diagram (using a variation of OMT), but I've redrawn this structure in Figure 6 using UML.

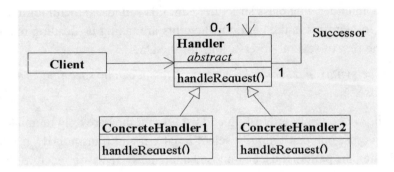

Figure 6. Class diagram showing chain of responsibility structure.

This figure shows a class named Client, responsible for initiating request, together with a hierarchy of Handler classes. There is a one-way association from the Client to the Handler.[24] Similarly, there is a one-way association from the Handler to its successor. As the multiplicity adornments of this association indicate, every Handler may have exactly zero or one successor, and every successor has exactly one Handler. The Handler class is abstract (so noted by its property). In this Figure, I've shown two potential sub-classes.

Gamma goes on to describe the dynamic semantics of this pattern through both a message trace diagram and an equivalent object message diagram. In Figure 7, I've redrawn this as a UML collaboration diagram.[25]

---

[24] This is an update from the 0.8 documentation on UML: We've settled upon the directed line as the means of showing the direction of an association. A solid line with no arrows is a bidirectional association.

Figure 7. Collaboration diagram showing a chain-of-responsibility scenario.

So, to specify this mechanism, Gamma has some descriptive text, a scenario, and an underlying class structure. Hm: this sounds an awful lot like a use case. In fact, this is the path our thoughts are taking us, leading me to suggest the first of several observations for the UML:

> *The syntax and semantics of a mechanism can be specified as a use case.*

Patterns are certainly interesting and useful, but they are only templates. In other words, one can't simply select a pattern and transmogrify it into code. Rather, the pattern must be imposed upon the systems architecture, and adapted to the context of that domain. This is what generative patterns are all about. For example, suppose you are building a MIDI controller.[26] Typical MIDI events include key presses and controller events (such as a user pressing a foot pad or turning a pitch bend dial). Primary clients thus include keyboards (or their equivalent) and controllers (which are either discrete or continuous), which mainly request note on/note off actions. These requests might be handled by a chain of MIDIEventHandler classes, with the lowest classes in the chain handling the most common events (note on/note off) and

---

[25] [In asking Grady for clarification, he explained that the role with respect to a pattern is conceptually equal to role on the association, although the precise semantics are not forced to be the same in UML. A role is the face something places upon the world. (This definition came from Kenny Rubin, in his Object Behavior Analysis method defined while he was at Parcplace.)]

[26] MIDI stands for Musical Instrument Data Interchange, a standard format for communication among digital musical instruments. MIDI has somewhat revolutionized the electronic musical instrument industry, making it possible for artists to mix and match input devices (e.g., keyboards, MIDI-enabled flutes, sequencers) with various sound generators (e.g., samplers, FM synthesizers, drum machines), all from different manufacturers. This example, in fact, comes from a real project: Together with one of my musician friends, I'm building a MIDI controller for a hammered dulcimer.

the higher classes handling more complicated events (system-exclusive messages).

In practice, I find developers who say "I'm going to use pattern *x*" and then shape their classes so that they conform to this pattern. However, the fact that this pattern was used is typically left in the developer's head instead of being explicitly recorded as a design decision. That's fine for the short term, but as the architecture evolves and as staff turns over, that decision will fade from the project's memory.

Since the use of a pattern constitutes an important architectural decision, it makes sense to explicitly show the presence and the use of certain patterns. Figure 8 suggests one possible solution.

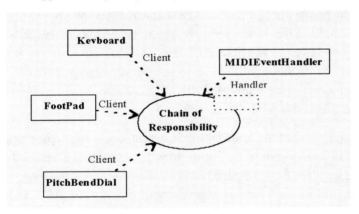

Figure 8.

Class diagram showing conformance to a pattern.

This figure is a class diagram, containing four classes (`Keyboard`, `FootPad`, `PitchBendDial`, and `MIDIEventHandler`) and one use case (representing the mechanism `Chain of Responsibility`). This kind of diagram can be distinguished from a use-case diagram, which consists mainly of use cases and actors (which are drawn as stick figures). In Figure 8, I've indicated conformance to the `Chain of Responsibility` mechanism by the use of the UML dependency relationship, adorned with the role the class plays. Thus, we can read from this diagram that the class Keyboard conforms to the pattern `Chain of Responsibility` and in fact serves as a `Client` class in the context of this pattern.

This suggests another observation for the UML:

> *Conformance to a mechanism can be indicated on a class diagram by a dependency upon the use case that specifies the pattern.*

This particular approach achieves two important things: first, it permits a team to explicitly record the decision to use a pattern, and second, it provides enough information for generation of that pattern in the context of the classes that conform to it. Zoom inside the use case, and you find the specification of the pattern; look at the classes that conform to the pattern, and find its generated instance.

Let's radically change the example, and turn to a common mechanism found in middleware technologies such as CORBA and OLE. Both CORBA and OLE adhere to a publish-and-subscribe mechanism. In other words, certain services *publish* their interfaces, and others *subscribe* to them. Additionally—and especially in a distributed system—there might be many concrete implementations of that published interface. Thus, when building an OCX component (such as one might do with Visual Basic or Visual C++), one assumes the use of this publish-and-subscribe protocol.

Ah: notice I've used the term *protocol*. A protocol is in essence a pattern of collaboration among objects. For example, the protocol whereby I make a phone call involves me lifting the receiver, waiting for the dial tone, dialing the number, and waiting for the other party to pick up. CORBA and OLE conform to a publish-and-subscribe protocol (actually, they conform to a number of interrelated protocols). So, another observation:

> *A protocol is a pattern of collaboration, just like a mechanism, and so can similarly be specified as a use case.*

Contracts are a related concept. Wirfs-Brock defines a *contract* as "... represent[ing] a list of services an object (a client) can request from another object (a server) (Wirfs-Brock et al. 1990)." Similarly, Jacobson and his colleagues refer to this same idea in their work.[27] However, I take a bit more dynamic interpretation than does Wirfs-Brock: a contract specifies a (static)

---

[27] Jacobson, I., Bylund, S., Jonsson, P., & Ehneboom, S. (1995). Using contracts and use cases to build pluggable architectures. *Journal of Object-Oriented Programming, 8*(2).

set of services together with a (dynamic) specification of the ordering of those services. For example, consider the protocol of a stack: it provides push and pop services (the static semantics), but you must push an item on the stack first before popping it (the dynamic semantics).

In UML, we already have a means of showing a contract through the use of an interface. By attaching a suitable property to a class, we can mark it as just an interface. This begins to serve the case of which Wirfs-Brock speaks, which is the specification of a list of services. If we add to this a state machine (already a part of the semantics of classes in UML) we thus have a means of specifying the dynamic semantics of a contract.

Now, let's combine these ideas of contract and protocol. For example, in Figure 9, we show the modeling decision that the class Customer (a concrete class from some problem domain) depends upon the contract OCX-Client (an interface in the OLE context), which in turn conforms to the OLE Publish-and-Subscribe protocol.

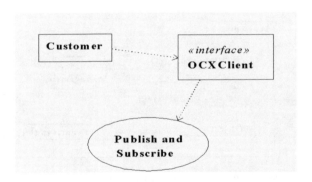

Figure 9. Class diagram showing contracts and protocols.

Figure 9 represents a simple case, the presence of a single protocol. However, I alluded to a more pragmatic problem above: complex frameworks such as CORBA and OLE present a multitude of services and a number of protocols for properly using those services. This is in fact the problem I raised in my last question, "what does this mean for specifying the semantics of frameworks?"

As I defined it earlier, a framework is a microarchitecture. Statically, one might package the elements of a framework (such as MacApp, the Microsoft Foundation Classes, or a CORBA ORB) into a UML package or packages. That handles the static case. However, how can we specify the protocols associated with that framework? Stated another way, how can we specify the mechanisms that framework uses? Stated yet another way, how can we specify the tabs and slots and knobs and dials that clients use to bolt their system to a framework?

Here's a hint to a possible solution: Packages can export classes, so why not let them export mechanisms as well? Thus, a possibility for UML:

> *The pluggable semantics of a framework can be specified as mechanisms exported by that framework.*

For example, consider the fragment class diagram in Figure 10:

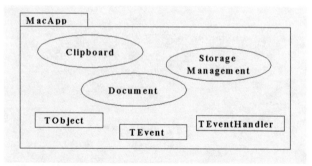

Figure 10. Class diagram showing framework semantics.

This Figure shows a single package named MacApp. This package exports a number of classes, only a few of which are shown, such as TObject, TEvent, and TEventHandler. Similarly, the framework defines and exports a number of mechanisms, such as Clipboard (which defines how applications can cut and paste to a clipboard), Document (which defines how applications interact with the file system), and Storage Management (which specifies how applications seize and free resources from the operating system). We must specify these as mechanisms, because they represent behavior that results from the collaboration of several objects. Furthermore, by explicitly

176

exporting these (and other) mechanisms, we record the information necessary for clients to properly use this framework, rather than mucking through a veritable mass of operations.

So, let's go back to my original question: In modeling an object-oriented system, how can I represent the use of a pattern? Our possible solution turns out to be a simple one: Patterns, protocols, mechanisms, and contracts all seem to be related to the semantics of the use case. Furthermore, with just a clever reuse of existing UML concepts plus some additional semantics, we get lots more expressiveness: the ability to make patterns first-class citizens in the modeling language.

CHAPTER 7

IMPLEMENTATION

Over the years, Grady has dealt with the specific mappings between his method and a variety of programming languages. The Booch notation's rich semantics, for example to express visibility and concurrency, have made it especially popular for designers. Although he is best known for his books on Ada and his second edition (1994) with its C++ examples, he has also written on other languages. We present a few of these here:

- In *The OO Languages*,[1] Grady describes what makes a language object-oriented and summarizes the OO language landscape as it was in 1994. Grady discusses how C++, followed by Smalltalk, were the most pervasive object-oriented programming languages and states (in 1994) that he would be surprised if this would change. This was, of course, written before the advent of Java and the thought of an OO Visual Basic.

- *The Design of Reusable Class Libraries* describes how OO can help achieve reusable code, and provides examples in C++. Grady discusses tactical language issues, strategic design issues, and their relationship to reuse.

- *Object-Oriented Development with Visual Basic*[2] describes how large-scale VB applications can be successful and benefit from an OO approach. Although Grady has seen some failures with VB and warns that one must proceed with caution, he remains optimistic about VB's future.

---

[1] Based on Booch, G. (1994). Coming of age in an object-oriented world. *IEEE Software,* 11(6).

[2] Based on Booch, G. (1996). Object-oriented development with Visual Basic. *Object Magazine, 5*(9).

- In a second VB article, *You Need a Software Recycling Program,*[3] Grady describes the often wasteful development practice of building software components that cannot be re-used. He encourages development organizations to adopt strategies of recycling and reuse. He discusses current and, one hopes, future language-support features that enable these strategies.

- *Development of the Web, by the Web, and for the Web*[4] discusses how the Web changes the nature of software development. He presents industry trends and practical advice on how teams can use the Web during development to improve team communications.

- *Java.*[5] In the hype of the Web and Internet explosion, Grady describes Java's role in creating distributed applications, and how developing a meaningful Internet application still remains a fundamentally hard software engineering problem. Grady describes how OO abstractions help and describes mapping from Java to the Booch and UML semantics.

THE OO LANGUAGES

In the haze of marketing hype, one is easily led to believe that anything good is object oriented, and anything object oriented is inherently good. Rubbish. Some of the worst applications I've seen, as well as many of the most profound and elegant ones that I've encountered, claimed to be object oriented. Happily, I find statistically more good than bad object-oriented architectures than I find among nonobject-oriented ones.

---

[3] Based on Booch, G. (1996). You need a software recycling program. *Visual Basic Programmers Journal, 6*(7).

[4] Based on Booch, G. (1996). Development of the Web, by the Web, and for the Web. *Object Magazine, 6*(6).

[5] Based on Booch, G. (1996). Object-oriented development with Java. *Report on Object Analysis & Design, 2*(6).

What is and what isn't object oriented has a reasonably sound litmus test. Simply stated, object orientation involves the elements of *data abstraction, encapsulation,* and *inheritance with polymorphism.* If any of these elements are missing, you have something less than an object orientation.

Object-oriented programming is where most developers are first exposed to the technology. With well over one million C++ compilers shipped worldwide and with more and more APIs being written in object-oriented languages, it is difficult for the up-and-coming developer to avoid object-oriented programming. By my count, there are close to 100 programming languages that can truly be called object oriented. However, most of these are research languages, not production-quality ones with the support of a full suite of tools. Of course, making judgments about any programming language is fraught with danger, but at the risk of offending every language zealot, let me suggest that, of this 100, only a small number of such languages are currently suitable to widespread, production-quality development.

For a variety of technical and social reasons, C++, followed by Smalltalk, are the most pervasive object-oriented programming languages. It is likely that this situation will not change in the coming years, but only become more entrenched over time.[6] C++ has developed a relatively easy following with organizations that are already experienced with C, as well as with projects that want to take the plunge in object-oriented technology, but want to do so with a language that is perceived to be dominant and thus has a large infrastructure of tools, APIs, and educational collateral. Smalltalk has developed a sizable following in a number of vertical domains, most notably in the financial community and in client/server architectures wherein Smalltalk is typically used to address the client side of the model. For many Smalltalk applications, the tight integration of the language and its tools is a major factor in the decision process of projects for which time to market and resilience to change are the dominant issues.

C++ and Smalltalk will likely have different evolutionary paths, however. ANSI and ISO standardization for C++ is underway, and already future fea-

---

[6] [Keep in mind that this was originally written in 1994.]

tures for the language have been and continue to be managed through a relatively well-defined process. Most production users of C++ currently work with what is called version 2 or 3 of the language definition, with future upward-compatible definitions bringing in such features as exception handling, run-time type identification, name-space management, and standard class libraries. In the case of Smalltalk, the language itself has been relatively static for some time, and it is in the realm of its supporting class libraries that we will see movement, particularly as different application frameworks are created. A striking difference that exists between C++ and Smalltalk today, however, is that the C++ environment is relatively tool poor, whereas Smalltalk is relatively tool rich. Part of this difference is cultural ("give me a compiler and a place to stand, and I'll move the world!"), and part of it is an issue of maturity (Smalltalk the language has always been virtually indistinguishable from Smalltalk the environment). As time unfolds, however, we are beginning to see more sophisticated tools for both languages, and the fact that the demand of C++ tools is high makes this an especially attractive market for tool vendors. Opportunities for sophisticated programming development tools abound. For example, Visual/C++ provides wizards that serve to remove the tedium of certain programming tasks. There are also a few efforts underway to provide incremental compilation technology in C++. For both C++ and Smalltalk, development environments that are sensitive to the issues of large-scale software development will continue to mature.

Although C++ and Smalltalk may be winning the minds of more developers than any other language, this is not to say that all other object-oriented programming languages are inconsequential. In the category of most elegant, I place Eiffel, which has a vocal following, especially in Europe. In the most trusted-for-complex-systems category, I place Ada95. Many of the worlds next-generation air-traffic control systems are being written in Ada, for example (and as a frequent flyer, I'm very comfortable with that fact). Ada95 brings Ada fully into the object-oriented world, with the addition of inheritance with polymorphism. In the most flexible category, I place CLOS. In the most curious-and-waiting-to-see-what-happens category, I place object-oriented COBOL. Adding object-oriented features to COBOL gives this crusty yet durable language more staying power, although more than a few MIS organizations that I encounter are quite happy to purge themselves of anything that smells of COBOL, even if it is object oriented.

With regard to this spectrum of object-oriented programming languages, it is fairly clear that your children and your children's children will be maintaining some of the C++ and Smalltalk code that some of you are writing today. A frightening proposition, indeed, but it shows that, even in an object-oriented world, some things do not change.

THE DESIGN OF REUSABLE CLASS LIBRARIES

A major benefit of object-oriented programming languages such as C++ is the degree of reuse that can be achieved in well-engineered systems. A high degree of reuse means that far less code must be written for each new application and, as a consequence, means that there is far less code to maintain.

WHAT CAN BE REUSED?
Ultimately, software reuse can take on many forms.[7] We can reuse:
- Individual lines of code
- Classes
- Logically related societies of classes

Reusing individual lines of code is the simplest form of reuse (what programmer has not used an editor to copy the implementation of some algorithm, and pasted it into another application?) but offers the fewest benefits (because the code must be replicated across applications). We can do far better when using object-oriented programming languages, by taking existing classes and specializing them through inheritance. We can achieve even greater leverage by reusing whole groups of classes; we call such a collaboration of classes a class library. Cutting across application domains, a

---

[7] This is not meant to overlook the reuse of analysis and architecture, or the application of patterns.

number of different kinds of class libraries are possible, including libraries of foundation classes (such as the C++ Booch Components, Tools++, the NIH library, and libg++) and libraries for graphical user interfaces (such as C++/Views and ObjectWindows). Within vertical application domains, it is possible and economically desirable to craft domain-specific class libraries. Indeed, such frameworks are at the heart of many of the Japanese software factories, and, given the meteoric growth in the acceptance of C++, are emerging in domains as diverse as hospital patient care applications, securities and trading systems, and avionics systems.

TACTICAL LANGUAGE ISSUES

Tactically, C++ provides a number of language features that greatly facilitate the engineering of reusable software. Consider this elided declaration of a queue class:

```
class Network_Event...
class Event_Queue {
public:
  Event_Queue();
  virtual ~Event_Queue();
  virtual Event_Queue& clear();
  virtual Event_Queue& add(const Network_Event&);
  virtual Event_Queue& pop();
  virtual Network_Event& front() const;
  ...
};
```

Here we have a concrete realization of the abstraction of a queue of events, a structure in which we can add event objects to the tail of the queue, and remove them from the front of the queue. C++ encourages our abstraction by allowing us to state the intended public behavior of a queue, while hiding its exact representation.

Certain uses of this abstraction may demand slightly different semantics; specifically, we may need a priority queue, in which events are added to the queue in order of their urgency. We can take advantage of the work we have already done, by subclassing the queue base class and specializing its behavior:

```
class Priority_Event_Queue : public Event_Queue {
public:
  Priority_Event_Queue();
  virtual ~Priority_Event_Queue();
  virtual Event_Queue& add(const Network_Event&);
  ...
};
```

C++ virtual functions encourage our abstraction by allowing us to redefine the semantics of individual operations from a more generalized abstraction.

Under version 3.0 of the C++ programming language, we can craft even more general abstractions. The semantics of queues are the same, no matter if we have a queue of cabbages or a queue of kings. Using template classes, we may restate our original base class as:

```
template<class Item>
class Queue {
public:
  Queue();
  virtual ~Queue();
  virtual Queue& clear();
  virtual Queue<Item>& add(const Item&);
  virtual Queue<Item>& pop();
  virtual Item& front() const;
  ...
};
```

This is a very common strategy when applying template classes: take an existing concrete class, identify the ways in which its semantics are invariant according to the items it manipulates, and extract these items as template arguments.

Note that we can combine subclassing and templates in some very powerful ways. For example, we may restate our original subclass as:

```
template<class Item>
class Priority_Queue : public Queue<Item> {
public:
  Priority_Queue();
  virtual ~Priority_Event_Queue();
  virtual Queue& add(const Item&);
  ...
};
```

Type safety is a key advantage offered by C++ templates. We may instantiate any number of queue template classes, such as:

```
typedef Queue<char> Character_Queue;
typedef Queue<Network_Event> Event_Queue;
typedef Priority_Queue<Network_Event> Priority_Event_Queue;
```

... and the language will enforce our abstractions, such that we cannot add events to the character queue, nor floating point values to the event queue.

Graphically, we may represent the relationship of a template class (Queue), its instantiation (Event_Queue) and its instance (net_q) as shown in Figure 1:

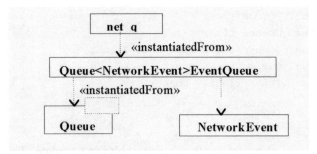

Figure 1. Class diagram showing instantiation of a template class and object.

STRATEGIC DESIGN ISSUES

Bjarne Stroustrup has observed that "designing a general library is much harder than designing an ordinary program (Stroustrup 1991, 429)." The design of any genuinely useful class library demands the delicate balance of

186

competing and often conflicting technical and social requirements. For example, consider the design of a foundation class library. As designers, we must consider the protocol of each abstraction from the perspective of at least two kinds of clients: the clients that use the abstraction (by declaring instances of it and then manipulating those instances), and clients that subclass the abstraction (to specialize its behavior). Designing in favor of the first client leads us to hide implementation details and focus upon the responsibilities of the abstraction in the real world; designing in favor of the second client requires us to expose certain implementation details, but not so many that we allow the fundamental semantics of the abstraction to be violated. This represents a very real tension of competing requirements in the design of such a library.

Additionally, we must consider a host of other issues, such as the library's
- time and space semantics,
- storage management policy,
- use of exceptions, and
- concurrency semantics.

Remember that in all nontrivial C++ applications, no class is an island, meaning that the design of one class must be done in harmony with all other classes: Classes must collaborate (because they share common protocols, such as for memory usage and for detecting and reporting exceptional conditions), and classes must share a common "look and feel" (otherwise, clients will have a difficult time understanding the semantics of individual classes that are part of a much larger class library).

CASE STUDY
Let's consider a few of these strategic design decisions, by studying how one particular foundations library addresses each issue.

The C++ Booch Components is a second-generation class library. The original library was written in 1984, and consisted of approximately 150,000 lines of Ada. In 1989, Mike Vilot and I redesigned this library using C++ for the Macintosh. In anticipation of the then emerging C++ features, we used templates and exceptions extensively. The next year, we ported the components to a variety of workstation-based compilers, and finally in 1992, we ported the components to Borland C++ 3.1, because it represented the first commercially available, production-quality C++ compiler that supported templates in meaningful ways.[8] [9] The current release of the C++ components consists of only 15,000 lines of code—and, we are discovering ways to make the library even smaller, with the same levels of functionality.

Why the dramatic different in the size of the libraries? We expect that by redesigning the original Ada library, now knowing what we do about patterns of use of the library, we could achieve perhaps a 20% or 30% reduction in the size of the library just by rewriting certain key abstractions. However, the biggest difference in the size of these libraries comes from the incredible economy of expression that is possible through the use of subclassing together with templates.

The library's approach to time and space semantics illustrates this point most clearly. In generalized foundation class libraries such as this one, we must recognize that different clients require different time and space semantics. For example, on a workstation that provides a large virtual address space, clients will often sacrifice space for faster abstractions; in certain embedded systems, such as in deep space satellites or automobile engines, memory resources are often at a premium, and so clients must choose abstractions that conserve scarce memory resources (for example, by using stack-based rather than heap-based representations). Still, it is desirable to have a common protocol for a class, no matter what its representation. C++ facilitates this idiom, through the use of pure virtual abstract base classes.

In our library, we have one base class for each major kind of abstraction, and then provide concrete classes by "mixing in" (through multiple inheritance) different kinds of representations. Graphically, we describe this design as follows in Figure 2:

---

[8] It is highly significant to note that across all these diverse platforms, there are absolutely *no* differences in the library's source code. The only difference among releases are the contents of the make files (since each platform uses slightly different make languages).

[9] The C++ Booch Components are commercially available from Rogue Wave Software, *http://www.roguewave.com.*

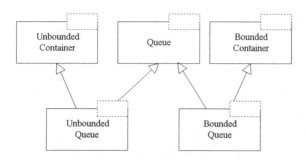

Figure 2. Class diagram showing 'mixin' inheritance.

The class `Unbounded_Container` provides a very efficient linked-list structure that uses items allocated from the heap; this representation is time-efficient, but less space-efficient (because for each item, we must also save storage for a pointer to the next item). The class `Bounded_Container` provides a very efficient, optimally packed array base class; this representation is space-efficient, but less time-efficient (because, when adding new items in the middle of the container, items at one end must be moved down by copying).[10]

In C++, we express this design of the Unbounded_Queue class follows:

```
template<class Item>
class Queue...
template<class Item, class Storage_Manager>
class Unbounded_Container...
template<class Item, class Storage_Manager>
class Unbounded_Queue :
  public Queue<Item>,
  private Unbounded_Container<Item, Storage_Manager> ...
```

[10] Our library actually provides a third representation, called Dynamic_Container, which uses a dynamic array representation. This representation provides a balance of time and space semantics, which is useful for many kinds of applications.

Thus, the Unbounded_Queue is a kind of Queue, but uses the Unbounded_Container for its representation.

Note also the template argument Storage_Manager. We provide this argument, so that clients can fine-tune the storage management policy for each class. Recall that in C++, it is possible to provide new and delete operators for each class. This idiom is often far better than relying upon the global new and delete operators, because, knowing the representation of a class, it is possible to provide a far more efficient storage manager (the most common form of which manages larger pools of memory that are pre-allocated chunks at a time). A client can then instantiate the Unbounded_ Queue by providing a storage manager class that conforms to the following protocol:

```
class Storage {
public:
  static void* allocate(size_t s);
  static void deallocate(void* p, size_t s);
};
```

In this manner, our class library does not make any assumptions about the storage management policy used by any particular application. Instead, clients can tune the library to their particular needs, but without having to pay the price for overly generalized (and hence inefficient) foundation classes.

In a similar fashion, a general class library must consider the problems of concurrency. Currently, there is no approach to lightweight processes defined by C++ itself. However, in operating systems such as Unix, OS/2, and Windows/NT, applications may be formed using multiple processes. Unless special consideration is given, most classes will simply not work in such an environment (when two more tasks interact with the same object, they must in some manner cooperate to avoid corrupting the state of the object). Again, we can use templates to generalize the problem. In our library, we further specialized the unbounded, dynamic, and bounded classes as follows:

```
template<class Item, class Storage_Manager, class Semaphore>
class Guarded_Unbounded_Queue :
  public Unbounded_Queue<Item, Storage_Manager>,
  private Semaphore...
```

We use the Semaphore class as the agent responsible for providing mutual exclusion on the object (meaning that different tasks interacting with the same object don't conflict with one another); through its superclass Unbounded_Queue, the guarded form has the same protocol as all other classes.

CONCLUSION

Building simple classes is hard. In crafting general class libraries, one must trade off flexibility and simplicity. Strive to build flexible libraries, because you can never know exactly how programmers will use your abstractions. Furthermore, you must build libraries that make as few assumptions about their environment as possible, so that programmers can combine them with other class libraries. Balancing this requirement for flexibility, you must build simple abstractions so that they are efficient, and so that programmers can understand them. The most profoundly elegant class will never be reused, unless the cost of understanding it and then using the class is lower than the programmer's perceived cost of writing it from scratch. The real payoff comes when your abstractions get reused over and over again, meaning that others can get leverage from your hard work, and so focus upon the unique parts of their particular problem.

OBJECT-ORIENTED DEVELOPMENT WITH VISUAL BASIC

"What this?," you may ask. Is there a typo in the title? Did Grady's mind encounter an "abort, retry, fail" condition? Even worse, has he renounced all things object oriented and been drawn over to the world of the <shudder> *nonobject-oriented* programming language???

Actually, it's none of the above. Let me explain by way of three observations:

First, there is much more to object-oriented stuff than just object-oriented programming. Object-oriented analysis and design methods can be applied to a variety of programming languages, object oriented as well as nonobject oriented. Projects typically apply the Booch Method when targeting to C++, Smalltalk, or Ada, but I've encountered a number of projects implementing in COBOL, Pascal, plain old C, and yes, even Visual Basic (VB). Moreover, I've encountered projects using my method for nonsoftware domains, such as the modeling of patient health care processes and the modeling of organizations. In short, object-oriented analysis and design methods are not necessarily bound to object-oriented implementations.

Second, for VB in particular there is no denying its presence and the fact that multitudes of projects are experiencing reasonable degrees of success with it. As for its pervasiveness, I'm told that the two millionth copy of VB shipped recently. While in New York, I worked with a company that had used VB for a large order-entry system; while in Taipei a few weeks ago, I worked with a government organization using VB for a large inventory control system. Now, I'm not claiming that all two million users of VB have been wildly successful. Indeed, I've seen some pretty dramatic failures—but more on that later, for it strikes at the heart of why the marriage between OO and VB is important for both camps.

Third, while it is clear that Microsoft's VB 3.0 is distinctly not object oriented, VB 4.0 is at least object based, according to Peter Wegner's definition. VB 4.0 supports classes as well as mechanisms for encapsulation, which makes the language object based. VB 4.0 lacks inheritance and true polymorphism, which prevents the language from being classified as object oriented. Still, object-oriented methods can go a long way in helping build systems that are object based, as experience has shown. Furthermore, the reality is that many very complex systems are rarely homogeneous, but rather are built using a number of languages. In client/server systems, it's not uncommon to find C++ on the back end and VB on the front end, for example.[11] Building systems with a focus on the construction of an object-oriented architecture makes it possible to leverage these disparate technologies, while at the same time preserving a conceptual whole. Indeed, with VB's explicit support for three-tier architectures, together with the emergence of products such as distributed OLE, experience suggests that applying an architecture-driven approach is absolutely central to properly using these technologies.

Before I continue, let me point out that this discussion concerning the marriage of all things object-oriented with VB actually generalizes to a larger class of 4GLs, such as Powersoft's Powerbuilder and Gupta's SQL-Windows. While unique in their own right, each of these three products share one common characteristic: They facilitate the creation of GUI- and data-intensive systems by visual programming rather than by traditional programming. Each of these three products also share one common shortcoming: There are practical limits to the complexity of systems that can be crafted using these 4GLs. Now, don't get me wrong. I'm a major fan of VB, Powerbuilder, and SQLWindows. If I encounter a domain that fits well with any of these three, then I'm the first to recommend their use, for writing traditional code when you don't have to is a pretty stupid thing to do.

To explain what I mean by this practical complexity limit inherent in 4GLs such as VB, let me point out that I see two common failure modes when this limit is hit. First, there are tactical constraints manifest in the languages themselves that make it difficult to scale up. Returning to the VB-based order entry system I cited earlier, I failed to mention that the company ran into an unforeseen problem shortly after they deployed the system. After about two months of operation, the 32,768th order arrived... and the system promptly failed, for internally, this became the order number -1 (and then -2, -3, and so on). Second, there are systemic constraints manifest in the lack of any kind of architectural support in 4GLs such as VB. Returning to the VB-based inventory control system I cited earlier, I failed to mention that the project is in somewhat of a downward spiral, because the team is afraid to

---

[11] In fact, we've built such a mixed-language system at Rational to manage our internal repository of documents.

change anything, owing to the fact that the system they built is particularly fragile. Most likely, they will have to scrap what they've built when the next round of new requirements comes in.

This systemic constraint is particularly onerous, because of the seductive nature of VB. There is no doubt that time-to-market can be accelerated by using languages such as VB. There is no doubt that it is easy to do flashy things quickly by using languages such as VB.[12] However, projects that start small often find a way of growing big quickly (since each new feature is always "just a simple matter of programming"), and yet this systemic lack of architectural support means that your house of cards can collapse around you at the most unsuspecting and most awkward time. Stated another way, this technology is great, but it sometimes has the side effect of amplifying human limitations and thus enabling projects to fail more quickly and more sensationally then they could have in the past.

As Figure 3 illustrates, in the domain of MIS systems, we find a range of applications, from those that are user-centric to those that are data-centric. As I stated earlier, if your system's requirements lie at one end of the spectrum or the other, then it is generally profoundly foolish to write traditional code. For example, if your application consists entirely of scraping data from an existing relational database and presenting it to the user in a flashy way, then by all means use a GUI builder. Similarly, if your application consists entirely of pumping data into a repository (such as with checkout scanners at a supermarket) then by all means use a database builder.

---

[12] Time-to-market and strong support for visualization are benefits often cited in the context of Smalltalk, but notice here that I'm discussing Visual Basic. I'm not trying to take sides, nor am I trying to fuel any religious debates, but let me suggest that Visual Basic is perhaps the greatest threat to the future of Smalltalk.

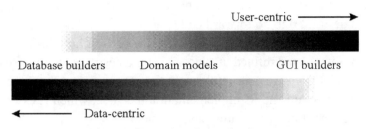

Figure 3. Forces in software development.

However, these solution options fail to scale if your application lies somewhere in the middle, because neither GUI builders nor database builders address the management of a system's domain model.

Put another way, 4GLs such as VB work especially well if the following two conditions are met: first, there exists a tight connection between the application's data and its visualization and second, all interesting data has a direct visual metaphor whereby it can be manipulated. If your system meets these two conditions, VB alone is right for you. If your system has characteristics that step outside either or both of these conditions, then you will likely experience the two meltdown modes I described earlier, unless you do something to mitigate that risk. I should point out that with VB 4.0, the opportunity for building more complex systems of this nature is greater, since VB now supports the creation of classes (such as "customer" or "order," as well as the reificiation of business rules that dictate how these classes collaborate) that do not necessarily have a simple or direct visual analog.

So, what is that "something" that mitigates this risk? That something is the use of object-oriented techniques to control a project's architecture, from which we employ the 4GLs to their best advantage, namely, GUI and database building. This means using object-oriented analysis to specify and bound the desired behavior of the system, and using object-oriented design to model the domain and its business rules. In practice, scenario-based analysis works wonderfully in this context, because it helps to develop a common vocabulary for the domain model, as well as almost optimally capturing the interesting and important interactions users have with user- and data-centric systems. Similarly, using notations such as class diagrams, state

195

machines, and object diagrams are particularly useful in expressing the structure and behavior of this domain model. From this model, it is then possible (and desirable) to do forward code generation into the 4GL, and then using the 4GL to "paint" windows and databases. Similarly, as the implementation is tuned and refined, it is possible (and desirable) to reverse engineer this model from the 4GL implementation. By so doing, the project can keep the architecture and its implementation in synch, which is essential if this is to be more than just a throw-away system.

This approach works because it provides a means for the project to control the system's architecture. (It really does: I've been on a number of engagements using VB, Powerbuilder, and SQL/Windows, among others, that have effectively used this strategy to control the architecture of their products and to extend the scale of these 4GLs.) Without this control, it is easy to build fragile applications in VB, because the knowledge of behavior and business rules get scattered throughout the system.

Organizations will continue to employ languages such as VB, because its entry cost is perceived to be low and its payoff is perceived to be high. Many such organizations will be successful in small projects that employ not one whiff of object orientation. Many such organizations will fail miserably in large projects, largely because they failed to use object orientation to its advantage. This is why I speak of the marriage of object orientation and VB. It is not an unnatural union, because there really is a methodological fit between the two. Moreover, it's a union that can and should flourish, because it leverages the benefits of each, while mitigating the weaknesses of each as well.

YOU NEED A SOFTWARE RECYCLING PROGRAM

Faced with the specter of an unstoppable deadline rushing toward you, individual developers will take whatever action is necessary to beat their code into submission before that deadline arrives. This is a very human response, but in the worst case, it means making compromises that you may later regret: Corners can be cut, algorithms may turn out to be less than perfect, and the architecture will likely become patched in unnatural and inelegant ways. For the individual developer and for the project as a whole, this always looks like the Right Thing To Do in the short term, because—or so the reasoning goes—there will always be another chance to clean up things. Besides, meeting the schedule is always the most important consideration, right?

Well, that's sort of true, up to a point. Just like a business, it's false economy to always optimize for the short term at the expense of the long term. Heroic programming is never a sustainable software development practice: at the end of the day, you might be meeting your early schedules, but ultimately your people and your project will reach meltdown. First, relying upon heroic programming is a great way to burn out your best people. Always having to write expedient code rather than good code is never rewarding in the long run. Second, you end up with a lot of software scrap. An oft-patched system will over time become so fragile that if you touch it in one place, it falls apart in another. When that happens, developers begin to pile patch upon patch and so in the worst case, no one can understand the resulting system.

One of the cool things about Visual Basic is that it greatly lowers the entry cost to writing user-intensive software. That's a good thing, because it means that VB has made it economically feasible to automate a whole new class of problems on a very wide scale. VB 4.0 further pushes the envelop of what's possible by offering advanced facilities for rapidly and easily building distributed systems.

However, small and simple systems have this nasty way of growing up to be large and complex systems. Thus, if your development organization is focused on the short term, you'll wake up one day to discover that you have a ravenous software monster on your hands that you must constantly feed with a steady stream of programmers. That creates a huge opportunity cost, because it means that you end up spending lots of resources keeping your system alive. Furthermore, adding new features becomes incrementally more difficult over time. Often, the only recourse is to discard the system and start over.

A far better strategy is a policy of *reuse* and *recycling*. Notice that I call this a "*policy*," because it is something that must be institutionalized by the software development organization as a whole. Writing a component for reuse is incrementally more work than writing it for one specific context and hence, in the short term, simple economics discourages this practice. However, across the organization as a whole, reusing a good component is far less work than writing one from scratch. There is unfortunately a difficult social issue that compounds the problem: Developers typically will overestimate the cost of finding and reusing a component, and underestimate the cost of building a suitable component from scratch. Hence, there's a balance that must be maintained: spend the resources necessary to develop components for reuse, but don't over-engineer them such that you don't get any real work done.

Another cool thing about Visual Basic is its notion of *components*, which are the quintessential reusable part. Again, VB 4.0 raises the bar by making it possible to write domain-specific components that model elements of some business, and often don't have a visual analogue. Getting these kinds of components right the first time is generally impossible, which is why I encourage software recycling, not just reuse.

Recycling says that you take something and transform it over time into something even more useful. If you've got an incremental and iterative development process in hand, that this means that you can build a components for the short term yet allow yourself the opportunity to improve that component with each new release. Thus, recycling is not exactly pure reuse (since the components is transformed) but neither does it require the more radical action of discarding it entirely (think of recycling as discarding the bad parts of a component just a little bit at a time). This is precisely what I've seen in the most successful VB shops I've encountered: a focus upon architecture, which concerns itself with the structure of configurations of components, not just the individual components themselves, and a focus upon an iterative and incremental life cycle, which allows the architecture and its components to mature over time.

How does one institutionalize a policy of recycling? There are a handful of practices I encounter in hyperproductive organizations.

- *Design components for an 80% solution.* In other words, do design your components with reuse in mind, but never strive to accommodate all possible situations. Not only is a 100% solution impossible (the best components are always domain specific and thus cannot be crafted in a vacuum) but that last 20% is exponentially more expensive to achieve. Furthermore, you simply can't *a priori* design a component to be reusable: The best components are evolved in the context of real use. There's a rule of thumb that Rebecca Wirfs-Brock uses, that says that it takes at least three tries to get a framework right.

- *Focus on crafting collaborations of components, not just individual ones.* This is a lesson that's hard to grasp at first, but I find it in all of the most productive organizations. Interesting components never work in isolation, but rather, always work in collaboration with others. For example, what's your architecture for dealing with exceptional conditions? How are transactions manifested? Do you have a common mechanism for logging? These are all architectural considerations that cut across many components. Thus, it is best to explicitly architect these decisions, so that the many different components in your system have a conceptual integrity.

- *Lower the cost and raise the benefit of recycling.* Once your project starts reaching a modest size (i.e. more than a couple of dozen components and/or more than two or three developers) it's best to organize a simple repository so that people can find the components they can reuse. In my experience, simple solutions are better than complicated ones. You might do something as simple as having internal Web pages that announce the presence and location of new components. In larger organizations, I've seen management encourage reuse by selecting a "component of the month" and rewarding its author with a small token (for example, a 6-pack of Jolt or a dinner with his/her significant other, whom they've probably been too busy to spend time with because of the deadlines in the first place).

Far be it from me to tell Microsoft what to do, but there are some things that would help VB encourage greater recycling. First, how about real support for inheritance? VB 4.0 is a class-based language, meaning that it supports abstract data types but not inheritance of subtypes. Inheritance helps greatly in building a family of components, because it facilitates the generalization of abstractions and their specialization. Second, how about a facility for specifying and visualizing collaborations of components? Staring at a component in isolation is a pretty painful way to begin to understand it. A far better way is to browse the patterns whereby that component interacts with other components.

So, am I implying an object-oriented Visual Basic? *Indeed I am.* VB has grown up to be a language that a number of organizations have used to build systems upon which they bet their business. Since those problems and business are only getting more complicated, there's good reason to let VB grow up to better support componentware in the large.

DEVELOPMENT OF THE WEB, BY THE WEB, AND FOR THE WEB

Depending upon to whom you listen, the Web changes everything, or the Web changes nothing.

I think it changes some things.

One cannot deny the unprecedented growth of Web traffic. Network Wizards reports that the number of Internet hosts will grow from about 4.85 million to 9.47 million during 1996.[13] The Business Research Group reports that 11% of all U.S. corporations were running intranets last June, and they expect this figure to grow to over 50% by June of 1996. The number of users

---

[13] "The Net on the Edge" *Information Week*, April 29, 1996. Several other statistics and quotes are drawn from this article.

who can access the Web is hotly debated, but whatever number you choose, it's still on the order of several millions.

So, the development *of the Web* is uncontested. Market forces are propelling the Web to becoming a pervasive force in computing. There will be some winners in this market and there will be some dramatic losers, but ultimately, it will change they way all of us in the software profession do business. As *Information Week* also points out, there will be some setbacks along the way, particularly as net traffic continues to overwhelm available bandwidth. Personally, this seems to me to be mainly an issue for the public Web. Private intranets have greater control over their network topology, and in addition are in a better position to manage their return on investment in Web technology.

John Whiteside is general manager of the IBM Global Network, and he observes the same phenomenon when he notes that "more people are going to be driven to private intranets where they can control the network behind the firewall." This is where a lot of dramatic growth of the Web is happening. At Rational, for example, we have both a public Web site[14] which we use to communicate with our customers, as well as a much larger private intranet that we use to communicate across our offices. When I need to find out information about the latest release of a product, obtain the minutes from some meeting, get some help configuring a new piece of software, or track down a technical paper, I just go to our intranet. In many ways, our private Web helps to preserve Rational's corporate memory, with very low overhead.

Development *for the Web* is the domain of such things as HTML, VRML and Java. Suffice it to say that the underlying technology is changing, although not as fast as it was in early 1996. HTML has undergone some much needed improvements, VRML seems to be taking hold, and Java seems to be moving beyond its initial period of hysterical excitement and into a period of consolidation and maturation. Although I've not seen any compelling uses on the public Web, I am beginning to see some compelling uses of Java for private intranets.

---

[14] *http://www.rational.com.*

Every software technology seems to require a "killer app;" that's what I mean by having a compelling use. Java helps to make distribution transparent, and that for me is the nature of Java's killer app. If you think about it for a moment, the Web has simply brought us back to the computing model of the '60s: dumb terminals attached to distant mainframe computers. To navigate the web, we interact with browsers that are little more than screen scrapers that slowly reach across communication lines to touch a distant networked computer. What's different from the '60s model of computing is that today we have color bit-mapped terminals, and the mainframe is essentially the entire world.

Today also, the majority of Java applets do little more than bring a little of that distant computational power to the screen, in the form of dancing heads and bouncing balls that liven up a page. What I'm now seeing are applets that bring some value to the client side of client/server architectures. What's now starting to emerge are applets that exploit the pervasive distribution of the Web, in the form of agents that move about the networked computer. That is where the killer app for Java resides.

Something else that is compelling about Java is that it offers machine independence, although at a cost. However, as long as network latency dominants the equation of response time, the execution cost of Java will remain tolerable. Furthermore, all of the major platform vendors have recently announced that they will directly support the Java Virtual Machine in their operating systems, and this over time will vastly reduce Java's performance cost.

Unfortunately, as I write this article [in early 1996], we are still at the level of banging rocks together insofar as Java development tools go. This comes to me as no surprise, for the Java phenomenon is tracking almost exactly the same path of maturation as did Ada and C++.[15] Happily, here again, market forces are at work to resolve this limitation. Java tools are getting better

---

[15] My, this makes me feel old. In just the last decade, I've been through three major programming language revolutions: Ada, the first engineered class-based language, C++, the most widely accepted object-oriented language, and now Java, the first language for the Internet. What's interesting is that the time between each new language is getting shorter and shorter.

faster, largely because much of the lessons learned from C++ development environments apply to Java.

In the context of development for the Web, here's one thing that the presence of the Web does not change: building safe, reliable, predictable, and useful systems that are both distributed and concurrent is still very hard. If anything, Java and the whole Web phenomenon make distribution pervasive and transparent and so raise the bar of complexity. So, my observation here is that we don't expect Java to make software development for the Web easier: it's intrinsically a wicked problem.

Development *by the Web* is a concept that I've only seen a few brave souls try to put into practice, but that I expect more and more to exploit over time. Frankly, I'm writing this article to point out that there is a tremendous value to be gained by using an intranet to manage the products of development. Many have suggested the use of central repositories to hold the artifacts of development. In a very real sense, the Web itself acts as one massive repository, and furthermore one that is fully distributed, nonproprietary, and capable of holding any kind of artifact, either existing or not yet imagined.

To better explain how an organization might do software development by the Web, let me walk through a few common use cases, the first involving pulling artifacts from the Web, and the second pushing artifacts from the Web.

> *Pulling: Finding the latest release of a framework* — Here I am working on the next development release of a product. Yet another version of the Microsoft Foundation Classes has arrived. I get an e-mail message saying its available, and so I go to an appropriate page, from which I can download it to my machine. If for whatever reason I need to fall back to an earlier version, I can find it there as well.

> *Pulling: Reviewing a design* — I'm assigned to develop a new feature. First, I write a concept document, which I publish on the Web. I point my colleagues to it, and they can read it online before we do a design review. After the review, I polish the document, and put it back on the Web so that there's an accessible statement of what was agreed upon. As I implement that feature, I might generate models

using my favorite analysis and design tool, and publish them on the Web. My colleagues can pull this information from the page to study it. If my modeling tool is well-integrated with the Web, they can click on a model in a page and then be brought to the tool directly, thus letting them browse the models in ways that a static page presentation does not permit. Once this feature is implemented, the artifacts of this design remain in the Web, as part of the project's memory.

Pulling: Evolving a use case — After working with a domain expert, I've got a better understanding of a specific use case that shapes the behavior of the system I'm building. As I did to review a design, I'll model this use case in my favorite analysis and design tool, and publish some scenarios on the Web so that my colleagues can more easily refer to them. As my thinking evolves, I may whip up a simple prototype, which I deliver as an applet or as a helper application. Either way, anyone studying that use case can look at the appropriate Web page and get to the associated prototype directly.

Push: Establish the results of a build — My development team has synchronized its work, we've checked in our last changes, and thrown the release over the wall to be built overnight. As part of the build process, regression tests are run. The results of the build, and the results of the regression tests, are packaged up, and a new Web page is generated by the build tools. When the team returns to work, they can visit the appropriate page to see how the build went. Looking at releases over time, management can look at this history of release information to see trends and take appropriate action.

Push: Drive user feedback directly to the appropriate developer — As customers use the product, feedback will come into the organization in the form of e-mail and calls to the support center. This information is pushed into a bug-tracking system, which in turn can push summaries out to new Web pages, custom generated for each team member. In addition, defect discovery reports can be pushed out to an appropriate Web page, thus offering a real-time instrument panel that measures the health of the project.

There are several more push and pull scenarios that come to mind, but this should give you a basic idea of what is possible.

Development *of* the Web is certainly accelerating. Development *for* the Web is slowly maturing. Development *by* the Web is a concept whose time has come.

JAVA

Hardly a day goes by that I don't read some article extolling the wonders of the Internet. A recent cover story in *Business Week* observed that "the Internet changes everything."[16] Various reports from Sun Microsystems and Netscape predict an explosive growth in commerce on the Internet. Studies suggest that, among certain age groups, people are spending more time surfing the Web then they are surfing channels on cable TV. Perhaps most telling, the Internet is squarely on Microsoft's radar screens; judging by Bill Gate's reaction to developments in this area, the Internet poses the greatest challenge to the company's future.

Notwithstanding all the hype, however, there is real substance here. I grew up on the ARPAnet starting around 1980, so e-mail and international networking are like breathing to me. However, two things have made the Internet even more compelling: the emergence of the World Wide Web, together with the law of increasing returns as applied to pervasive net-working. The Web, initially developed at CERN to facilitate communication among a small community of high-energy physicists, has grown to transcend all national boundaries and now offers a dizzying selection of content. The laws of increasing returns, a twist upon the old economic theory on the law of diminishing returns as applied to tangible products, says that for every new connection to the Web, its value grows. Thus, as long as infrastructure

---

[16] The Software Revolution. (1995, December 4). *Business Week*, p. 78.

keeps up with the demand, the Internet has within itself the means to flourish and to fuel its own long-term growth.

The Web has subtly and materially changed the way I work. Like many others, Rational has its own home page, which we use to present our product offerings and to disseminate technical information.[17] Internally, we use it to keep our worldwide field appraised of relevant collateral and late-breaking information. (It's this kind of use that's threatening the business case behind Lotus Notes, for example.) I've begun to use the Web to document the unified modeling language, largely because of the Web's unsurpassed ability to manage hyperlinks among evolving content. On a more personal basis, I've used the Web to order components for a robot,[18] to check on the local weather for a forthcoming vacation,[19] and, perhaps most importantly, to become a member of Dilbert's ruling class.[20]

So, *Business Week* is correct in the sense that the Internet changes everything, at least from the perspective of the content consumer. However, they are very wrong about one thing: developing meaningful applications for the Internet is still a fundamentally hard software engineering problem.

Let me explain. For the most part, building Web pages today is largely a matter of using HTML. This is part technical (HTML is a fairly classical markup language) and in a large part is artistic (crafting inviting and approachable Web pages requires a sense of esthetics and novelty). There is much that one can do using basic HTML.[21] However, as Ed Yourdon points out, "for the most part, the Web has been a mechanism for publishing static content for end users to leisurely browse,"[22] the emphasis here being on the word *static*. Ed goes on to note that "the Java phenomenon has changed the

---

[17] *http://www.rational.com.*

[18] *http://www.activemedia.com.*

[19] *http://www.satlab.hawaii.edu.*

[20] *http://www.unitedmedia.com/comics/dilbert.*

[21] Furthermore, tools are emerging to make HTML writing even easier, such as the free filter that converts Microsoft Word documents to HTML, as well as Adobe's Pagemill, which permits drag-and-drop creation of Web pages. In the very near future, the emerging standard of VRMTL will accelerate the development of three-dimensional worlds on the Web.

[22] Yourdon, E. (1996). Java and the new wave of Internet programming languages. *Corporate Internet Strategies, II*(1),1.

nature of application development completely." This is for two reasons: Java facilitates live HTML, and Java changes the granularity of components that comprise an Internet software system.

It is not my intent here to provide a tutorial on Java; not surprisingly, far more complete information is available on the Internet itself.[23] Suffice it to say that Java is fundamentally a programming language simple enough to get value from quickly, expressive enough to dress up static Web pages and make them dance, and yet powerful enough to serve as the vehicle for building some serious, industrial-strength distributed systems. Java is a true object-oriented programming language, which I describe as being a little like C++ minus all the baggage from C, blended together with some ideas from Objective-C (dynamic binding), Smalltalk (automatic garbage collection and pointerless programming), Cedar (lightweight, pervasive multi-threading), and Ada (a consistent type system). From a conceptual perspective, objects in Java are all active and distributed. That makes Java a natural for building applications for the Internet. Furthermore, Java's concept of applets facilitates platform interoperability (the Java Virtual Machine executes portable bytecodes, in the same way that, eons ago,[24] UCSD Pascal used p-code to achieve portability), provides a better locality of reference (since applets execute on the client, not the server), and discourages bloatware (since Java systems are not monolithic, but rather are formed from collaborating societies of applets.

Developing meaningful applications for the Internet with Java is still fundamentally a hard software engineering problem, simply because engineering large, multithreaded, distributed systems—no matter what the implementation technology—is fundamentally a wicked problem. Building simple, sequential applets will be a snap. In fact, I expect that the creation of applets for live HTML will fuel a cottage industry of the same magnitude as did OCXs for Microsoft's Visual Basic. However, building large systems is a hard problem in its own right. Building correct multithreaded applets is hard, but not an intractable problem for anyone with a little computer science sense. Building efficient and effective distributed systems on the bleeding

---

[23] *http://java.sun.com.*

[24] In software years. Eighteen months calendar time is roughly equivalent to one software *eon.*

edge of the industry's software engineering abilities is also hard. Put all of these characteristics together—large, multithreaded, and distributed—and you've go a problem that's exponentially harder than just building a large or multithreaded or a distributed system.

I offer this warning because I see in Java a phenomenon I've seen too many times before: simple systems that work well have a nasty way of evolving into big systems that sputter and breakdown and collapse of their own sheer weight. Furthermore, try to scale development techniques that work well for simple systems, and you'll fail: the sustainable development of large, complex systems requires fundamentally different techniques than heroic programming efforts offer. It's not that these large system development techniques are unknown. In fact, the good news I'm offering here is that we as a maturing industry have a reasonable handle on a number of solid software engineering principles: object orientation is good, architecture-driven development is good, incremental and iterative life cycles are good. The even better news I offer here is that these techniques apply directly and beneficially to Java.

Given this context, I and my colleagues have set about to couple Java to the Booch Method and, ultimately, the UML. Herein I have more good news: We have found that there is a natural fit between Java and these object-oriented analysis and design (OOA/D) methods. This coupling is relevant because experience shows that solid OOA/D is essential to visualizing and engineering the architecture of complex systems. There is only so much one can grok (i.e., understand) by perusing the linear text of a piece of software. The Booch Method and its successor, the UML, permit one to visualize a number of alternate yet integrated views of a large, multithreaded, distributed system. By forming a path between the artifacts of these methods and Java, it permits both the forward and reverse engineering of Java and facilitates multiple, integrated views of the system under development: the logical and physical views of an architecture from the perspective of the OOA/D artifacts, and the code view from the perspective of the Java applets.[25]

---

[25] There is precedence for this coupling. Specifically, we have mapped the Booch Method to C++, Smalltalk, Ada, Visual Basic, Gupta's SQLWindows, and Powersoft's Powerbuilder, as well as a number of other fourth-generation languages.

In describing this mapping, I'm assuming that the reader has a basic familiarity with the features of the Java language.[26]

PROGRAM STRUCTURE

A compilation unit in Java maps to a module in the Booch method. Packages in Java serve both a logical and physical means of decomposition, and as such map to isomorphic categories and subsystem in Booch. Furthermore, the Booch concepts of visibility and dependencies relative to categories directly support the Java concepts of namespaces and importing.

CLASSES

Java classes map directly to classes and utilities in Booch. Utilities in Booch map to a Java class whose attributes and operations are all adorned as static. The Java visibility modifiers public, protected, and private all map to identical properties in the class specifications of Booch. Attributes and aggregate relationships in Booch map to fields in a Java class declaration. For these attributes, the Java modifiers static, final, transient, and volatile all map to equivalent attribute or aggregation properties in Booch. Operations in Booch map to methods in a Java class declaration. For these methods, the Java modifiers static, final, abstract, native, and synchronized all map to equivalent operation properties in Booch.

Constructor and finalize methods in Java map to code-generation properties in Booch.

INTERFACES

Java reifies the concept of an interface to separate type[27] and class hierarchies. In Booch, interfaces map to simple classes by convention, distinguished by setting an appropriate class property that marks this entity as an interface only. In the UML, interfaces (and protocols) are first-class citizens, and so there exists a direct mapping to and from Java interfaces.

---

[26] *The Java language specification, Version 1.0 Beta* (1995). Sun Microsystems.

[27] [Java's use of the term *type* is somewhat non-standard compared to other languages.]

RELATIONSHIPS

Java provides classical single inheritance through the interaction of the "extend" and "implements" relationships, both of which map to inheritance in Booch.

Associations in Booch are higher level modeling concepts than those found in classic programming languages, and thus are derived from the more primitive features of Java. For example, a simple association in Booch may be mapped to mutually referencing objects in Java.

THREADS

Java's semantics encompass lightweight threads, together with a variety of synchronization primitives such as guarding statements (which define a critical region of expressions) and synchronized methods (which provide a lock on a per-class or per-object basis). Statements and expressions in general are treated as language-specific elements of Booch, and so there is a one-to-one mapping. Synchronized methods in Java map to guarded operations in Booch.

Applets reify threads. Thus in Booch an active object maps to an applet. In the UML, threads and processes are first-class citizens, which thus map more directly to applets.

DISTRIBUTION

In Java, applets aren't necessarily aware of their location. From a systems modeling perspective, however, architects must consider the physical distribution and migration of entities. In Booch, such distribution is modeled by convention in object diagrams (or UML collaboration diagrams, which may show migration) and process diagrams (or UML deployment diagrams, which serve to specify distribution). In the UML, the location of an entity is one of its predefined properties, and thus there exists a direct way of showing both the distribution and the migration of an object in an collaboration diagram. Furthermore, the semantics of Booch process diagrams have been tightened in the UML, permitting a more self-consistent model: the allocation of threads and processes (and other entities) may be visualized directly in the UML deployment diagram, and use cases coupled to collaboration diagrams may be used to show the prototypical mechanisms of distribution and migration of Java applets, classes, and objects.

PREDEFINED PACKAGES

An essential part of the whole Java culture is the existence of a number of predefined packages, including java.lang (providing the declaration of a number of fundamental classes), java.io (the moral equivalent to standard I/O in UNIX), java.util (the moral equivalent to the standard template library in C++),[28] and java.awt (a simple windowing framework). These frameworks map to categories in Booch (and packages in UML). Furthermore, and especially so in the UML, use cases may be tied to these packages, for the purpose of specifying the mechanisms (and thus the behavior) carried out by these packages. This approach is one we've taken to extract the patterns in libraries such as Microsoft's MFC and Borland's OWL, so that a more abstract architecture may be presented to the developer.

Let me be clear that mapping Java to the Booch Method does not involve any rocket science. This is largely because Java embodies a lot of classical object-oriented features, and because the Booch Method (and the UML more so) are expressive enough to cover a wide variety of modeling issues.

It is possible to build good Java applications without any of this object-oriented stuff? Certainly. An amazing number of applications in many different languages have been built by various world-class developers using the most primitive of software development tools. Does this OO stuff help? A resounding yes. There simply aren't enough world-class developers around to satisfy the demand for good software, and furthermore, there are many problems with inherent complexity such that no amount of heroic programming hours will suffice. This is why when crafting Java systems, it is desirable to apply OOA/D to drive the development cycle. As this article shows, there's a good impedance match between Java and the Booch Method, permitting OOA/D in the front end to flow naturally to a Java implementation.

---

[28] At this date, Java has no provisions for template classes, although they are apparently under discussion.

ACKNOWLEDGMENTS

I thank David Tropeano from Rational Software, who devised the original Booch-to-Java mapping, and Guy Steel from Sun Microsystems, who helped to clarify the concurrency semantics of the Java language.

CHAPTER 8

LOOKING AHEAD

Here, we present an interview conducted with Grady in which he addresses what he anticipates for himself and for the industry.

Where are your efforts focused?

I'll be working on more collateral for the UML, helping to make it approachable. Although our work (meaning the work of Jim, Ivar, and myself) has been well received by those already using OO methods, reality is that there are even more developers not using any identifiable method. It is this audience that I most want to reach out to.

I usually spend about 30-40% of my time as an architectural consultant or mentor. This means that I work with companies trying to craft large systems and help them architect their software, as well as their organizations. This work keeps me honest, true to my philosophy that you should never trust a methodologist who does not use his or her own work.

In the more distant future, I see myself continuing to push on understanding architecture and the notion of big architectural patterns. The work of Gamma and his colleagues lays a good foundation. Mary Shaw's work starts to address the issue of big architectural patterns, and this greatly interests me. This is akin to Microsoft's work with line-of-business objects.

What do you see as your role in popularizing OO and UML?

I've been evangelizing OO before OO was cool…. My first paper came out on the topic in 1982,[1] and ever since I have been pushing the technology. Languages and technologies come and go, but OO-ness seems here to stay. As for the UML, it will succeed (or fail) on its own technical merits. I don't want to explicitly popularize it, but I do want to help people understand and

---

[1] Booch, G. (1982). Object-oriented design. *Ada Letters, 1*(3).

use it effectively. If UML helps people solve complex problems, it will need no artificial popularizing.

When do you expect UML to stabilize?

People are already using it on projects. Some of the earliest involve projects at U.S. Customs, the IRS, and in the NYC Criminal Justice System. Do realize that the UML really is the natural successor to Booch, OMT, and OOSE. Thus, in many ways it is already stable. At the time the 1.0 version is released to the OMG, the UML will have already had widespread usage.

What will happen to the Booch Method?

If I were starting a new project, would there be a reason not to use UML? There is really no reason to continue using Booch, OMT, or OOSE in the presence of the UML. For early adopters, the key issue will be the availability of trained people and good tools, but over time, say after mid-1997, this will become a moot issue. The macro and micro processes are, of course, still applicable.

What is your view on the future of process?

Well, the future of process is inevitable ;-). Seriously, there is great attention in the issues of process today, and that is a good thing. However, there is a strange situation here: successful organizations tend to have good processes, but organizations that chase after good processes are not necessarily successful. This is why I have a love/hate relationship with things like the SEI CMM.

I think that over time we will begin to have a better understanding of the nature of processes. This is what I was writing about in *Object Solutions*. Still, software development is, and will continue to be, both an art and a science, so there must be room for creativity even in the face of rigid processes.

Also, it's not just process in isolation…. One must consider the interplay of people and architecture. All things being equal, I'd pick a group of *good people* over a *great process* any day. However, if you want sustainable, economic software development, then you have to consider all three: *process, people,* and *products.*

What do you think endorsement of UML from companies like Microsoft and HP have meant to the industry?

Both Microsoft and HP have customers who are using their products to build more and more complex things. Both companies have realized that modeling is important to break through that wall of complexity. Thus, their endorsement of the UML is a sign of the maturation of the industry as a whole. The fact that they have chosen the UML indicates that they realize its value in helping people build complex things.

How should people entrenched in structured techniques and committed to relational database technology best take advantage of OO and the UML?

Increasingly, systems are built with a database element, and often that element is highly distributed. We have taken great care to make sure that one can reconcile traditional RDBMS technology with OO systems. Thus, the UML is technically well-suited to this domain. Structured techniques are slowly fading away as organizations realize the value of object technology. As I explained in *Object Solutions,* the canonical solution to de-align with legacy methods and systems is to apply a thin object layer over them. This way, one can preserve older approaches while still moving to newer, object techniques.

What are the software industry's greatest challenges related to methods?

The rate of change in the software industry makes it difficult for people to absorb that change and take advantage of it. Thus, most organizations are just keeping their heads above water, so one can hardly even think about anything more than pushing software out the door. Thus, the greatest challenge to method and to process is convincing people that it will add value now, not just later.

Do you believe that UML is adequately suited to business process engineering? I can think of objections that may prohibit its adoption: "The notation does not look like what I learned in business school," and "how do I model the workflow of a business process?"

Ah, but the rules of business engineering are changing… It's a distributed, concurrent, heterogeneous, *net-world* out there, and so the classic business school approaches to software are woefully out-of-date. The UML is very well-suited to this domain. I've seen it used already to model the Justice System, processes in an HMO, and the business of Cable Systems. So, you can debate this, but reality is that there are existence proofs out there. The UML does work for business engineering.

What lessons-learned about software development do you anticipate to be shared between industry segments, for example, between telecommunications, defense, aerospace, and commercial?

This industry *is* so segmented. Furthermore, people who are doing good things in one industry are usually busy working on the next great piece of software, so the last thing they have time for is to write about it or even read about another domain that appears to be unrelated to what they are responsible for. One of the great opportunities I personally have is to see across all these industries on a worldwide basis. I'm struck by three common themes:
- Software development is hard.
- No one has the secret to making it easy.
- Complexity will continue to increase.

If anything, I think that there is a growing belief across all domains about the importance of two things:
- Process is good.
- The future is object oriented.

These shared beliefs will help defragment the industry.

On a personal note, it has been very satisfying to be a part of making object-orientation a mature technology that has helped teams deliver industrial-strength software.

REFERENCES

Alexander, C., Ishikawa, S., Silverstein, M., Jacobson, M., Fiksdahl-King, I., & Angel, S. (1977). *A pattern language.* New York: Oxford University Press.

Alexander, C. (1979). *The timeless way of building.* New York: Oxford University Press.

Bapat, S. (1994). *Object-oriented networks.* Englewood Cliffs, NJ: Prentice Hall.

Booch, G. & Bryan, D. (1994). *Software engineering with Ada.* (3rd ed.) Redwood City, CA: Benjamin/Cummings.

Booch, G. (1987). *Software components with Ada: Structures, tools, and subsystems.* Redwood City, CA: Benjamin/Cummings.

Booch, G. (1991). *Object-oriented design with applications.* Redwood City, CA: Benjamin/Cummings.

Booch, G. (1994). *Object-oriented analysis and design with applications.* (2nd ed.) Redwood City, CA: Benjamin/Cummins.

Booch, G. (1996). *Object solutions: Managing the object-oriented project.* Redwood City, CA: Addison-Wesley.

Brooks, F. (1975). *The mythical man-month.* Reading, MA: Addison-Wesley.

Chidamber, S. & Kemerer, C. (1991). *Towards a metrics suite for object-oriented design.* Phoenix, AZ: OOPSLA'91.

Chidamber, S. & Kemerer, C. (1993). *A metrics suite for object-oriented design.* Cambridge, MA: MIT Sloan School of Management.

Coad, P. & Yourdon, E. (1991). *Object-oriented analysis.* (2nd ed.) Englewood Cliffs, NJ: Yourdon Press.

Firesmith, D. & Eykholt, E. (1995). *Dictionary of object technology: The definitive desk reference,* New York: SIGS Books.

Foley, M. & Cortese, A. (1994, January 17). OS vendors pick object standards. *PC Week.*

Gamma, E., Helm, R., Johnson, R., & Vlissides, J. (1995). *Design patterns: elements of object-oriented software.* Reading, MA: Addison-Wesley.

Goldstein, N. & Alger, J. (1992). *Developing object-oriented software for the Macintosh.* Reading, MA: Addison-Wesley.

Grady, R. (1992). *Practical software metrics for project management and process improvement.* Englewood Cliffs, NJ: Prentice Hall.

Goldberg, A. & Rubin, K. (1995). *Succeeding with objects: Decision frameworks for project management.* Reading, MA: Addison-Wesley.

Harmon, P. & Taylor, D. (1993). *Objects in action: Commercial applications of object-oriented technologies.* Reading, MA: Addison-Wesley.

Jacobson, I., Christerson, M., Jonsson, P., & Övergaard, G. (1992). *Object-oriented software engineering.* Wokingham, UK: Addison-Wesley.

Jacobson, I., Ericsson, M., & Jacobson, A. (1994). *The object advantage: Business process reengineering with object technology.* Wokingham, UK: Addison-Wesley.

Jones, C. (1994). *Analysis and control of software risks.* New York, Englewood Cliffs, NJ: Prentice Hall.

Kruchten, P. (1994). *Software architecture and iterative development.* Santa Clara, CA: Rational Software Corporation.

Levy, H. (1984). *Capability-based computer systems.* Bedford, MA: Digital Press.

Love, T. (1993). *Object lessons: Lessons learned in object-oriented development projects.* New York, New York: SIGS Books.

Lorenz, M. & Kidd, J. (1994). *Object-oriented software metrics.* Englewood Cliffs, NJ: Prentice Hall.

Martin, J. & Odell, J. (1992). *Object-oriented analysis and design.* Englewood Cliffs, NJ: Prentice Hall.

Meyer, B. & Nerson, J. (1993). *Object-oriented applications.* Englewood Cliffs, NJ: Prentice Hall.

Orr, K. (1984). *The one minute methodology.* Topeka, Kansas: Ken Orr & Associates.

Pinson, L. & Wiener, R. (1990). *Applications of object-oriented programming.* Reading, MA: Addison-Wesley.

Rechtin, E. (1991). *Systems architecting: Creating and building complex systems.* Englewood Cliffs, NJ: Prentice Hall.

Rumbaugh, J., Blaha, M., Premerlani, W., Eddy, F., & Lorensen, W. (1991). *Object-oriented modeling and design.* Englewood Cliffs, NJ: Prentice Hall.

Schulmeyer, G. & McManus, J. (1992). *Handbook of software quality assurance.* New York, New York: Van Nostrand Reinhold.

Shaw, M. (1989). Larger scale systems require higher-level abstractions. *Proceedings of the Fifth International Workshop on Software Specification and Design.* (pp. 143-146). IEEE Computer Society.

Shaw, M. & Garlan, D. (1996). *Software architecture.* Englewood Cliffs, NJ: Prentice-Hall.

Simon, H. (1982). *The sciences of the artificial.* Cambridge, MA: MIT Press.

Shlaer, S. & Mellor, S. (1988). *Object-oriented systems analysis: Modeling the world in data.* Englewood Cliffs, NJ: Yourdon Press.

Stroustrup, B. (1991). *The C++ programming language.* (2nd ed.) Reading, MA: Addison-Wesley.

Tufte, E. (1983). *The visual display of quantitative information.* Cheshire, Connecticut: Graphics Press.

Walsh, J. (1992). *Preliminary defect data from the iterative development of a large C++ program.* Vancouver, Canada: OOPSLA'92.

Wirfs-Brock, R., Wilkerson, B., & Wiener, L. (1990). *Designing object-oriented software.* Englewood Cliffs, NJ: Prentice-Hall.

Yourdon, E. (1994). *Object-oriented systems design.* Englewood Cliffs, NJ: Prentice Hall.

LIST OF FIGURES

Notable Quotes

Page

2   To a young boy's active imagination, this was truly a thing of wonder.

2   Our ability to imagine complex applications will always exceed our ability to create them.

4   Indeed, I have seen the future, and it is object oriented.

4   For an endeavor as complex as crafting a large piece of software, the failure of any one aspect of a project can cause it to blow up in your face.

7   The dark side of this is that underdeveloped organizations tend to find sort of a moral anchor in the form of some really cool tool.

7   Perhaps finding some of their development efforts floundering, like a drowning man, they will grasp at whatever tool happens to float, only to find that faith in any one technical tool will indeed drag them down.

18   I do not view object orientation as the universal solution to the ongoing imbalance between software supply and demand.

27   Legacy code is like a dinosaur living in your office... no one in the organization may know exactly how it got there, but it's big, consumes mass quantities of resources to keep it alive, and demands attention.

34   It is relatively easy—but not free—to have locally high quality, as represented by individually crafted classes, so elegantly and cunningly fabricated they bring tears of joy to the user.

43   The object-oriented method wars regarding notation are largely over (long live the process wars!).

54   Measuring the rate at which pizza boxes accumulate outside certain programmer's cubicles may appear to have some correlation with rate of progress, but even that is not a very reliable measure.

66   An aside: Don't underestimate the importance of failure in object-oriented development.

71   Besides, who would pay money to see trained cows perform at Sea World?

80   We build models of complex systems because we cannot comprehend any such system in its entirety.

101   There is a political, personal, and technical unification taking place in the world of object-oriented analysis and design.

107   These are exciting times for the professional software developer, for this is still largely an era of innocence and unbounded opportunity. On the other hand, that's the worst possible news.

117   Scenarios do not by themselves define an architecture.

122   In all fairness, I must admit that there is a dark side to scenario-based development.

144   You shouldn't trust a methodologist who doesn't use his or her own method.

150   Provide a frank assessment on the state of the project. To do otherwise is to deny reality.

162   Not quite the excitement of bungee jumping or, perhaps even more intense, subclassing from a deep class lattice while mixing in a couple of other abstract base classes to achieve some desired polymorphic behavior...

180   In the haze of marketing hype, one is easily lead to believe that anything good is object oriented, and anything object oriented is inherently good. Rubbish.

180   Some of the worst applications I've seen, as well as many of the most profound and elegant ones that I've encountered, claimed to be object oriented.

196   Faced with the specter of an unstoppable deadline rushing toward you, individual developers will take whatever action is necessary to beat their code into submission before that deadline arrives.

207   Engineering large, multithreaded, distributed systems—no matter what the implementation technology—is fundamentally a wicked problem.

214   There must be room for creativity even in the face of rigid processes.

INDEX